Life STORIES

JAMES HASTINGS

G000054128

"Thank you, King James"

THE TOUGH LIFE OF ROBERT HICKS

How the King James Bible came to
the rescue of a boy from the slums

DayOne

© Day One Publications 2010

Reprinted 2012

ISBN 978–1–84625–232–7

All Bible quotations are taken from **the Authorised (King James) Version** unless otherwise noted. This version was in general use in the period when most of the events recorded in this book took place.

British Library Cataloguing in Publication Data available

Published by Day One Publications

Ryelands Road, Leominster, HR6 8NZ

☎ 01568 613 740 FAX 01568 611 473

email—sales@dayone.co.uk

web site—www.dayone.co.uk

Designed by Steve Devane and printed by Orchard Press Cheltenham Ltd

"In my career with the BBC, I have heard many fascinating stories of people's lives, but only two have struck me as worthy of a book. Robert's is one of them."
—Esther Rantzen, broadcaster and writer

"Robert's story, harrowing as it is, demonstrates that Someone is always listening and in sovereignty continues to surprise us all in the way He raises up individuals to be a blessing to many."
—Rev. Richard Bewes, All Souls Church, London

"Robert is a first-class honours graduate from the College of Hard Knocks. He is a testimony to the Christian principle that it is not where you come from but where you are going, that matters."
—Rev. Dr Steve Brady, Principal, Moorlands College, Christchurch

"Without individuals like Robert Hicks, movements like OM would be the poorer. I, for one, am inspired by him and his vision for the Word of God and its distribution."
—George Verwer, Operation Mobilisation

"Robert, I am always amazed by your vision and commitment to Jesus and his Gospel. Your many enterprises leave me speechless. Your life and testimony are an inspiration to us all."
—John RW Stott, Author, Bible scholar and rector emeritus of All Souls, Langham Place, London

Dedication

This book is dedicated to all children who have suffered at the hands of inadequate parents.

Thank you, King James records the remarkable influence that the King James Version (Authorised) Bible has played in the life of Robert Hicks.

First published in 1611 in the time of King James I of England, the year 2011 marks exactly four centuries that this version of the Bible has been in print.

Translated from the original languages of Hebrew and Greek by several godly scholars, it brought light and liberty of the English-speaking world as the power of the Word of God was unleashed, and the conscience of nations was touched.

Timeline

1941	Robert is born in Birmingham, the Midlands, the city of a thousand trades.
1941–1947	Lives in various care homes and with mother in Birmingham slums.
1947	Hicks family move to 335 Stonehouse Lane, Bartley Green. Father returns from the war.
Christmas 1947	Worst winter of the century
1948–1952	Robert attends two primary schools.
1951	His mother deserts family and Robert is sent to Middlemore Care Home.
1951–1956	Attends two different secondary schools.
1956	Robert becomes an apprentice grocer's boy at George Mason's and finally receives operation so he is no longer tongue-tied.
1957	Robert copies out and reads the Bible for the first time and comes to faith in Christ.
1959	Made Master Grocer, promoted to Relief Master.
1961	Robert and Joyce marry and he is appointed shop manager for the first time.
1973–1979	Marketing Director for the Co-Op in the North West. Launches UK's first hypermarket and also oversees 110 shops.
1979–1984	Becomes Publishing Director for Scripture Union. Leaves to start own publishing company in London.
1989	Joyce dies from cancer after two-year battle.
1991	Robert marries Annabelle.
1999	Robert publishes ten million Millennium Gospels.
2000	Joint promotions with the Daily Telegraph and the Daily Express.
2002	Robert conceives and sponsors *Back to Church Sunday*.
2009–2010	The *Fresh retelling of the Gospels* are published
2010	Robert publishes the Harper Collins *Bible Companion*.
2011	Celebrations planned for the 400th anniversary of the King James Bible. Launch of *Open Your Bible*—a new 800 page edition combined with a website www.openyourbibleresources.com.

Robert writes:

When I was a child, I found it nearly impossible to communicate with anyone outside my immediate family and a few friends who had learnt how to understand my peculiar way of speaking. As a result, I spent many hours every day thinking and reasoning within myself.

I would wander the fields around my house, holding conversations with imaginary individuals and imaginary conversations with real people. This, coupled with the developing powers of observation (something all children are blessed with), is the reason I have no difficulty in remembering those 'child's thoughts.'

At intervals in the book, some of these thoughts are recorded.

Robert as a young man, Bible in hand.

Prologue

For the first time fifteen-year-old Robert could remember, the blood seeping gently from his lip was not caused by his father's fist. The man, who would regularly beat his six children and abuse his daughter, was in his bedroom lost in a drunken sleep.

It was one o'clock in the morning, and the teenager sat alone in the kitchen. A single candle illuminated the starkness of the room which was like a textbook to poverty. An air of neglect hung on every bare wall; dust loitered on the floors and shelves, drifting into the empty cupboards. William Hicks spent his wages on booze and gambling and sometimes prostitutes, but not on his children. The drab kitchen at Number 335 Stonehouse Lane mirrored every other room in the house with the exception of the front room—that was where social workers and police officers were welcomed. It was kept immaculate.

Robert's mouth was still raw and tender from the previous day's operation. Every few minutes, a little blood swirled around the wounds where the doctor had removed a membrane from either side of his tongue, attaching it to the bottom of his mouth. The medical term was tongue-tied. It was a fairly routine operation, usually performed on an infant. But Robert's parents had never bothered taking any of their six children to their GP for regular check-ups, so the condition went undiagnosed; at fifteen, he underwent the procedure he should have received as a baby.

At school, Robert's poor speech led him to being labelled retarded. Combined with dyslexia, it was a difficult burden. His childhood was marked by constant worry and a searing loneliness and frustration. He felt adrift in a silent world; his brain knew how to speak, but his mouth was neutered. Robert's clumsy attempts to form words made other children giggle and adults impatient. One day in class, he raised his hand and asked a bemused teacher: "Dease sir, I need da doilet." So he simply did not speak unless it was absolutely necessary. His only release from his isolation was humming quietly to himself which annoyed everyone, especially his father; then the beatings followed, usually from father's old army belt. The huge, sharp buckle could easily tear open a child's skin.

Hospital staff were shocked a fifteen-year-old boy had turned up alone for such an intimate operation on his mouth. Robert did not try to find his father to go with him. He knew he would be entertaining a crowd in the local pub or gambling his son's wages away; mother had walked out on the family five years earlier and Robert had no idea where she was.

That night, using the wooden box which covered the gas meter as a table, he lifted his large pen, dipped the nib in some ink and took a piece of scrap paper he'd found in the grocery store where he worked. In 1955, speech therapy was not available on the National Health Service and, as his dad seized his wages every week, Robert had no means of paying for private treatment. The doctor who discharged the teenager made another suggestion:

"Robert, now we have removed the extra membranes, there's nothing to stop you speaking normally, once you get used to moving your tongue," he explained. "It's become flabby and weak with lack of use. I suggest you read out loud while writing the words down. That will help. Find a book, a large book, and copy it out by hand."

So that afternoon, Robert had searched every room at 335 Stonehouse Lane for a book, any book. He quickly realised the irony of his task. Finding a book in a house, which rarely had blankets on the one bed he shared with his four brothers, seemed a fruitless task. As he went from room to room, his frustration grew. After years of being called stupid, a retard, living in an isolated world, he finally had the chance to escape. He desperately wanted to speak and be understood. His need to express his true feelings, rather than just grunt emotions, was overpowering. He could not bear being stuck in his lonely grey world any longer. But first, he needed a book.

The one room he dared not search was the beast's room. That was what the children called their father's room. It was not a place to find things; it was a place where childhoods were stolen. It was where Robert's sister Jean was led in tears at night and from where she left the following morning in a stunned silence.

The one cupboard he dared not search was the one in the living room where his dad kept his army belt. But he had tried everywhere else, so finally, taking a deep breath, he pulled the door open. Plunging his hand into the darkness, he recoiled when he grazed the belt buckle. He pulled out a tin of shoe polish, a torn cloth and other rubbish. Then his fingers touched something softer. Dragging it out, he beamed when he saw it was a book. Dust and cobwebs shrouded the black leather cover. He was amazed to see the page ends were all in gold.

The book's title had faded so badly, it was unreadable. Taking a piece of shoe polish, Robert gently rubbed it into the cover, restoring the faded glossy sheen until it glistened. It was as if this book lit up the darkness. Placing it near his small candle, he gently turned the first few pages until he came to the first chapter. Lifting his pen, he scanned the first line and started to write, clumsily speaking the words out loud:

"In the beginning, God created the heavens and the earth."

Robert aged 11 with his mother on the day trip to Belle Vue in Manchester. Two weeks later, she walked out on the family.

A stranger calls

Robert Hicks was almost six years old when he was handed over to the woman he was told was his mother. Born in Birmingham in 1941, the first few years of his life were shared between different overcrowded houses and lengthy stays in a variety of care homes. Usually, he was sent away whenever his mother became pregnant, which was often. Winifred Hicks had ten children by four different men. Four of the children—including twins and a mixed-race girl—were placed for adoption before Robert ever met them. In later life, he thought about tracing these unknown siblings but had so little information he knew it would be hopeless.

Robert had no photograph of his mother and no mental image of what she looked like. His mother was almost a complete stranger. He could barely picture his sister and four brothers as they, too, were placed in different homes for months at a time. Sometimes, they would run away and come home themselves; other times it was the police who found them wandering around Birmingham.

"At home, it wasn't unusual for three of us to go to bed, and wake in the morning to find two new children sleeping beside us," says Robert. "These were my brothers, fetched from a care home late at night. This often happened when my parents needed extra social security money which was automatically reduced if children went into care. Of course, we never benefited from the money; it was used for a night out at the pub or new clothes for mother.

"Other times, I'd wake to discover one of my brothers was missing. He'd been taken in the night to a care home and it would be months before we saw him again. As children, we found it very difficult to bond as our time together was fractured; we were more strangers than siblings."

In the care homes, Robert's mother quickly became a distant memory, his father even more so. His mother never visited him in any of the care homes. When he was living in the slums, there was no mother-and-child bonding. This time, he had been placed in care because his mother was pregnant by another man, not her husband, and would soon give birth to a daughter Robert would never meet. The six Hicks children were left to look after themselves, especially at weekends when their parents spent all night in the local pubs or cinema. Before William Hicks was called up to the army in 1944, he had spent very little time with Robert or any of his children. After work, he would head straight to the pub. There were no visits to the park to kick a ball around with dad, no walking to school with mum or bedtime stories from either. When William Hicks was demobbed after the war, he eventually made his way back to his family. One afternoon, the six Hicks children—five boys and one girl—were placed before a handsome stranger standing in the kitchen dressed in a soldier's uniform and told: "This is your father."

Winifred was born in the slums of Birmingham but her grandparents kept her sheltered from much of the reality of that life. She had a love of fine clothes and regarded herself as different from the other slum-dwellers. Robert explains: "My mother was a strong, well-built woman who always felt superior to those around her because of the privileges she had received as a child.

"Like my father, she was overly attracted to the opposite sex and, like him, was incapable of accepting responsibility for her actions. She was educated and distinctive yet flawed, for mother was attracted to physically handsome men. She never bothered to discover their character but would quickly go off with them even if it meant staying out all night, leaving her children alone at home. She was only twenty-two when I was born, her sixth child. In all, she gave birth to ten children, but never became a mother. I have no memory of her ever hugging or kissing me unless it was to impress visiting social workers. Birthdays and Christmas went unmarked. I always felt like a trespasser in her presence. I longed to be touched, hugged and kissed. I wanted to be noticed and asked questions about school or who our friends were. But there was just silence born out of sheer disinterest.

"When she was at home, mother would sort her clothes or sit listening to the radio, anything but interact with her children. Looking back, the physical beatings from my father were extremely painful and terrifying. He could become furious at the slightest excuse then punch us or beat us with his huge army belt. However, the absolute indifference from both my parents, especially mother, to their children was probably more painful. They simply didn't care. We had no value, no relevance to their lives."

He adds: "It was like strangers using the same lift. You are aware of someone else's presence, but there is no conversation. You'll stare at the floor or a stain on the wall, anything but talk. When I saw other parents playing with their children in the local park, it was as if they were speaking a different language. Laughter, hugs and kisses were unknown vocabulary in the Hicks' house. Even today in my seventies, I find it awkward being hugged or kissed. Thankfully, I have now overcome this, although it has been hard."

Robert remembers the excitement of meeting his father after he was demobbed. He and his siblings idolised the man they could not remember, imaging him as a war hero, returning with exciting stories of bravery and daring, along with chocolates and chewing gum. Within days, however, the smiling soldier became the enemy.

"My father was born in Sheffield, Yorkshire, and, by all accounts, was a wild young man. It was rumoured he was forced to leave the city after getting a married woman pregnant and abandoning her. He had a punch-up with his mother before heading south to Birmingham where he met my mother.

"They married in 1939, when she was seven months pregnant with my older brother Jack and had a son, Donald, from a previous relationship, both born in the same year. Dad was tall, fit and handsome. He and mother were attracted sexually, but there was no emotional relationship. They could not remain faithful to each other.

"My parents loved drinking, socialising and the whole pub culture. At weekends, they would go out and have fish and chips before heading to the pub, while leaving only bread and lard or margarine for our tea. Their taste made me sick, but it was the only food in the otherwise empty cupboard."

Born just before an air raid

From an early age, the Hicks children learnt the futility of crying. Whether from hunger or in need of a consoling hug, any cry went unanswered. In Robert's case, the hard lesson began just hours after his birth. His mother had saved enough money to book into a private clinic, ensuring a room to herself. A cot for Robert was placed in the far corner.

A few hours after her baby was born, Winifred fell asleep. She eventually woke to the muffled sound of Robert's cries. Being tongue-tied meant his crying was different from that of other babies. But her son's odd whimpering did not concern Winifred. She was more alarmed the hospital was unusually quiet. She got out of bed and left her room, abandoning her son of a few hours alone in his cot. It would not be the first time Robert and his siblings were abandoned. Winifred walked along the empty corridor and down the main staircase until she eventually found the elderly caretaker.

He explained the staff and patients had fled the hospital after an air raid siren and were huddled in a nearby shelter. The hospital had been hit by bombs several times before, putting part of it out of use. Winifred had slept right through the commotion. When the staff finally returned, the nurses were embarrassed to hear they had left a new mother and her baby alone in her room.

"They fussed over mother for the next ten days," explains Robert. "I was taken out of her way so she could recuperate. It was the best time mother ever had.

"I had cried and cried in my cot but my mother did not come. She never came for any of her children. Mother had left me alone in an empty room in a deserted hospital. A normal mother's instinct would be to keep her child close to her at all times. The Hicks children knew crying was pointless. It elicited no response. We learnt that lesson very early."

Robert Hicks was born on the afternoon of Tuesday, February 26, 1941 in Handsworth. He weighed eight pounds and four ounces. All Winifred's children were heavy. Robert had the same soft creamy complexion as his grandmother, a fine head of hair and brown eyes. He was described as having a naturally happy face. Winifred had placed her three other children in the care of the Salvation Army, leaving her husband at home alone in the Birmingham slums. She knew he would have other women there while she was in hospital. She did not like it but accepted that was how their relationship worked.

After her ten-day stay was up, Robert's father sent a neighbour's twelve-year-old son to escort his wife and the new baby home to their rented rooms. She was helped on the

"I was born in a bombing raid, neglected in the slums, taken into care with no voice to speak. Not much to start life with."

train by a nurse while the boy carried her bags. William was unemployed at the time and could have fetched his wife himself, but chose not to. The Hicks lived in one of the worst parts of the slums. Houses backed on to one another and rubbish covered the streets. The few shops were mainly boarded up.

It was obvious other women had been living in the house while his wife was in hospital, but William made no effort to disguise the fact or to clean the place. The only provision he had made for a new baby was a cardboard box wedged between two chairs.

Robert has only negative memories of his six years in the slums: "There is a fashion today for collecting old sepia photographs of industrial Britain in days gone by. There are the inevitable images of boys wearing cloth caps, girls in aprons and horse-drawn wagons in the background. It is easy to look back on those days as simpler times, a bygone era of close-knit communities. The reality of the Birmingham slums could not have been more different. The slums were evil, foul-smelling places. They bred disease and utter despair. We shared a toilet with twenty other people. The stench was appalling. As children, we wandered around half-naked, urinating in the stinking puddles while dogs roamed furtively. Every Monday morning, gangs of housewives would scrub the steps outside their houses from the congealed human waste and vomit left by the weekend drunks. The overcrowding was so bad, father would often spend a few nights at a relative's house.

"The smell of the slums stayed with you wherever you went. My speech impediment meant I was trapped alone in this miserable existence, a prisoner to the stench of mankind. I could not tell anyone how unhappy I was, nor did any parents hug or comfort me and assure me everything would get better. Unable to communicate, I felt like I was experiencing it all from a distance, like watching a horror film, but, at the same time, trapped in the middle of the terror.

"In those conditions, incest was rife. Some children's first sexual experience in the slums was with a sibling or parent. My house was the ultimate stage-set of depravity. Incest, rape, perversion of all kinds, prostitutes and drunken brawls were all part of my childhood script. This was not a place for 'Winnie the Pooh' or 'Treasure Island'. Our house was an X-rated movie."

Robert's life soon settled into a pattern of neglect and abandonment. His brother Bernard was born twenty months after him, followed eighteen months later by Brian. This meant several stints in care homes. He was unable to bond with his brothers or other children in the homes because they never managed to be together long enough. Strangers flitted in and out of his life, so that "parent" became a word without meaning. Or rather, the only real meaning "parent" had was fear and misery and hunger and loneliness and beatings and abandonment and cold and despair.

In and out of care

It was a few days before Christmas 1946 when that despair came crashing into young Robert's life. He had been at the Erdington Cottage Home in Birmingham for several months. The Erdington was a large Victorian building with over a hundred children under care for various reasons. Robert vividly remembers the day he arrived after his mother announced she was pregnant again.

He said: "When she dropped me off, the great sadness I had was not that I was being separated from my mother, but that one day she would return to collect me. That was the pattern I had become used to. Just as I was enjoying having my own bed and regular meals instead of lard and stale

"I was her fourth child but she never knew my birthday. She never knew me. Not even for one day in a year."

bread, a member of staff would call me to a room for a chat. I knew that meant mother was downstairs and I had to leave.

"The staff at Erdington were friendly and tender. They did not punch or swear at children and they talked to us. For a few days, other boys had been thrilling me with stories about Christmas at the home. They told tales of cakes, sweets and presents and of a big bird that got cooked with hot food inside. When you are a child living in the slums, one of the most important things in your life is hot food. Every day I could smell new delights from the kitchen and marvelled at the colourful decorations and a real Christmas tree at the entrance. In my house, Christmas was never celebrated; my mother did not even know my birthday.

"Later I would learn this particular baby she was about to have was the result of an affair with a black man, which was a major scandal in 1950s Britain. When the baby, a girl, was born, my father demanded she was immediately put up for adoption. He already had one step-child living at home; he did not want a second one, a mixed-race child, living under the same roof.

"Being at Erdington was one of the best times of my life, yet I knew it could be snatched from me at any moment when my mother reappeared. I just didn't want it to happen before Christmas."

Two days before Christmas, a nurse called Robert over as he was playing with some other boys. He immediately knew, from the tone of her voice, this was the moment he had been dreading. He was about to be wrenched from a loving care home and handed back to his family. With a bright smile, the nurse said: "Robert, you are a lucky boy to be going home for Christmas. It must be better than being stuck here with all these children."

She had already packed his meagre bag of clothes. The nurse hummed a Christmas song as she combed Robert's hair then, taking him by the hand, escorted him along endless corridors until he felt cold air waft around his feet. He was one door from reception where the dreaded handover took place. He felt like a prisoner being returned from a relatively happy prison to the cold of a gulag. As the nurse pushed through this final checkpoint, Robert fought back tears.

There, leaning over the main desk, was a tall well-dressed woman signing some papers. She was wearing a warm winter coat and held her gloves in one hand while she went through the form with her pen. Beside her was a small girl, about seven; it was Jean. Her hands and feet were wrapped in newspapers, wet from the snow outside. Her thin coat was ripped at the back. She smiled but Robert did not respond. He was trying desperately to cling to every memory of the place where he had been so happy the past few months and not think about the slum where he was about to be taken.

The woman signing the forms did not look up. Robert knew it was his mother but he did not know her. She was barely thirty but looked older and tired. Then as he was pushed closer by the nurse, the little boy recoiled.

"My mother had a particular smell which always made me shudder," explains Robert. "It was not a lack of hygiene for she was prideful about her appearance. It was a smell that filled me with dread. I can't put my finger on it, but it was instantly recognisable after all these months."

The woman handed the form back to the receptionist murmuring a few words of thanks. Then she put her gloves on and straightened the bag on her shoulder. For the first time, she glanced at Robert. She did not bend down or smile or open her arms for a hug. With a twitch of her head towards the door, she gave an order as if talking to a dog: "Come on."

A 1940s Wolverhampton trolleybus, similar to those operated in Birmingham.

Storm clouds gather

As he squeezed through the heavy door of the home, Robert frantically scanned the snow-covered street looking for his mother. He spotted her crossing the road, dragging Jean by the hand.

"Hurry up, Bobby," smiled the little girl.

Robert's hands were blisteringly cold so he shoved them into his pockets but that made it difficult to run. Instead, he shook them in the frosty air as he chased after his mother. He was terrified of losing sight of her: she never once turned around in the street which was packed with Christmas shoppers. Robert was as cold inside, numb at the thought of returning to the slums. The smell and noise were already cluttering his senses and he cried some more. Just a few hours earlier, he had been playing with real toys, not broken ones found in the street; he had enjoyed an evening supper, giggling with other boys over tales of Christmas turkeys and presents. Now he was shivering, as he stood alone with his mother in a queue waiting to board a tram.

Robert was so cold he could not enjoy his first tram ride. His mother still did not talk to him but after a while, when she suddenly rose from her seat, Jean turned round to her brother:

"Our stop, Bobby. Get up," she whispered.

A few minutes later they boarded a big yellow bus which passed through Birmingham city centre. It was the first time Robert had ever been on a bus. The shops and streets were dazzling with Christmas lights, sights which made Robert twist and turn in his seat in awe. However, he quickly realised this was not the road to the slums, even though he was unsure exactly where he was heading. After half an hour, the bus conductress let out a yell: "Bartley Green."

When the bus drove off, Robert stood in a darkness and silence he had never before experienced. The slums were always crammed with people, noise and lights. This new place was empty and black. He had no experience of the countryside and was afraid of the shadows made by the overgrown hedges and trees. He strained to spot Jean waving to guide him as his footsteps echoed over the untouched snow. At last they reached a row of terraced houses, each with a small garden at the front. Their lights enabled him to see the Number 335 as his mother opened the door and an overwhelming smell of fresh paint struck his nose like a fist. Workmen had just finished decorating the house that afternoon and Robert's eyes watered as the fumes stifled the air.

Unsure where to go or what to do, Robert was rooted to the spot. He scanned his new surroundings. He was hungry, hoping for something to eat and drink after his journey. Instead his mother pointed to the stairs then snapped: "Up there. Bed."

In the first room he saw a large metal bed with a tattered mattress half-covered by a single sheet and blanket. A wooden chair was the only other furniture. Still wearing the clothes from the Erdington home, Robert crawled beneath the dirty blanket, crying uncontrollably until he eventually fell asleep.

At No. 335

The winter of 1946–1947 remains one of the coldest on British records. The windows at No. 335 were frozen shut by ice while snow drifted high against the back door from the fields behind, making it impossible to open. Bartley Green is now a sprawling housing estate and part of the city of Birmingham. But in post-war days, it was a tiny village surrounded by beautiful open countryside where people were thankful to live, happy to have escaped from the slums. The traditional terraced houses of Stonehouse Lane had recently been renovated by the local council. No. 335 had three bedrooms and an inside toilet but as the Hicks parents rarely spent any money on their children, they could not be expected to decorate the house. All the walls were bare except one in the living room where the previous owner had left a framed text in calligraphy. It read: "The Perfect Friend is one who knows the best and worst of us and loves us just the same."

Robert explains: "Jean read those words to me many times and they made me long for a best friend because Stonehouse Lane with its beatings and hunger, cold, poverty and dark secrets soon became a living hell. Everything in me rejected the pious sentiments of the text, yet I longed with all my heart it might be true. I felt the words both mocked me and gave me my one ray of hope.

"My mother's bedroom was in stark contrast to the rest of the house. She had a small wardrobe and a small but good collection of clothes. She also bought a chaise longue which she put in the sitting room. This item of furniture was something my mother had wanted since she was a child, although her children were not allowed to go near it. She brought it from our rented house in the slums. The neighbours gawped when they saw the extravagant piece, along with her nice clothes being loaded into a van.

"People nodded knowingly to each other. These items only confirmed what they believed, that mother had been running a

"I don't like the five of us sleeping in the same bed. I wish I had my own bed, like in the children's homes. Donald keeps most of the coat to himself and John keeps making wheezing noises. I was wet again this morning and I don't want to keep sleeping in this bed next to my brother who can't help wetting it. I wish I had my own bed."

brothel while father was away in the army and these luxuries were payment for services rendered. When I was older, mother denied the allegations but our family allowance alone could not have paid for all that she owned."

Winifred made several more trips into Birmingham to collect the remainder of her children. Over the next few days, Robert had to share his bed with his four brothers; Donald and John (who were both older than he was) and Bernard and Brian who had been in care in Wales. Jean had a room to herself.

Robert was uncertain why his mother had reunited the children: "It may have been because she was expecting dad home soon from the army or perhaps she was grieving after giving away her baby girl for adoption. It was more likely she wanted the family allowance which she could claim now we were all living under one roof again. It couldn't have been because she loved us. Mother had made no provision for her children in this new house. There was practically no furniture or toys. There were just two cups and a few plates for a family of seven. We drank out of old jam jars. We did not have knives or forks and always ate with spoons.

"We had even fewer clothes and, when our shoes started to come apart, mother gave us string to tie the uppers and soles together. If a hole appeared in the sole, we placed a piece of cardboard over it. When that failed, we wrapped old newspapers around our feet or went barefoot in the summer.

"The cold at night was the worst thing. Eventually, mum gave us one of her old coats which the five of us fought over in bed to keep warm. I soon discovered that if I put one leg down an arm of the coat, I could keep my share and sleep warm for the whole night. It was only when the weather was extremely cold that I was allowed to sleep in the same bed as mother and Jean. It was physically the closest point I ever was to my mother as she did not hug or cuddle her children. Jean recently told me about a fond memory she recalls from this time, when mother prepared a chicken Sunday roast occasionally, but I have no memory of such an event."

Out and about in God's creation

If inside No. 335 was like hell, then outside was like heaven. Green fields stretched as far as the eye could see, stumbling into rivers or bumping up against hillsides where wild apple and plum trees grew in abundance. Harvest time brought more bounty and the hay bales piled high by large tractors were transformed into castles. For the first time, Robert heard birds sing; he would follow insects of all types along little grass trails and gasped at flowers blossoming on roadsides and hedgerows.

His lack of speech made him a keen observer. People just smiled at the dirty-faced youngster sitting silently on gates and fences. But Robert soaked in everything. He learnt bird migration patterns, types of insects and animals. He studied the farmers at work in the fields and listened to them haggle with shopkeepers over prices; he scrutinised housewives and listened to their animated conversations; he was fascinated with the travellers and gypsies who visited in the summer.

The fields were a magical play area. A farmer kept his horses in a nearby meadow and the Hicks boys and their friends from the Stonehouse Lane Gang took turns riding them bareback. The strong horses immediately galloped off at the strange intrusion of a yelping child jumping on their backs. The boys clung to the animals' necks for as long as they could, before being tossed onto the soft grass.

One afternoon, Robert found an unexploded German bomb in a field. Not sure what to do with it, the Stonehouse Lane Gang decided to use it as a throne from where boy kings decreed what should happen to the great, the good and other neighbours of Stonehouse Lane. A few days later, a police officer arrived at the boys' den, asking if the rumours they had heard of a German bomb were true. When the startled officer saw a dirty-faced boy jumping up and down on the live device, he cleared the area with a piercing shrill of his whistle. Bomb-disposal experts arrived, the bomb was defused and the Stonehouse Gang were famous for a week.

Robert would spend long hours wandering alone across the fields, humming to himself. He found the rhythm soothing. Not being able to speak gave him headaches and humming released tension. He would practice talking to trees, cows and the bees flitting round his head on summer days. He hated being teased by children at school, but at least they noticed him. His mother rarely spoke to any of her children and never suggested a family walk or outing. It was during these long times spent apart in the countryside that Robert first began thinking about God.

He says: "In the Book of Romans, Chapter 1, verse 20, it states: 'For the invisible things of him from the creation of the world are clearly seen, being understood by the things that are made, even his eternal power and Godhead; so that they are without excuse.'

"I didn't know anything about the Bible or the churches. The only time I heard the name of Jesus was as a swear-word

"I like the buttercup and daisy flowers in the fields. They both have bright yellow eyes looking up, but they close at night time. I feel like the field flowers. When I am out of the house something inside me opens up as I walk the fields talking to myself. When I get home at night, something inside me closes down and all I can do is hum quietly to myself."

from the people in the slums. But like the Apostle Paul wrote in Romans, no one has an excuse for not knowing God through his creation. On my long walks alone, I'd often go to the nearby Frankley Beeches Reservoir and watch the reflections of the heavens in the water. Even at an early age, I would question the meaning of life and the universe itself. I knew there was something more than what I saw.

"One Sunday, a few of us went to the Sunday School at the local church. We heard they gave sweets to children. The people were very nice and I enjoyed the stories they told but although they talked about love, it was on their terms. I did not feel it extended to my life at No. 335 and what took place there. I did not understand why God could be interested in the life of every other creature on the planet except mine. Also, if God was as powerful as the Sunday School teacher claimed, why could he not transform my parents into a real mother and father like other kids had?"

During one of his walks, Robert came across an old Anglican church and noticed the door was open. Inside, he gasped at a gold cross on the altar and, in front, a beautiful painting of a man wearing robes, surrounded by people with wings on their backs. Hearing a voice, he quickly turned to see someone dressed in a long black robe with a white collar round his neck.

"How old are you?" asked the man.

"Dah'm deven," stuttered Robert.

"Do you like the paintings?"

"Dhes," replied Robert, embarrassed at the sounds he was making.

"The man in the painting is called Jesus," the man continued and he explained that the other people were angels. The man said Jesus liked telling stories. Robert listened to one about a farmer sowing seeds and another of a good shepherd and his lost sheep. It made sense, because Robert knew farmers and understood that those were the kind of things they did.

"Who is dis Jesus?" asked Robert.

"Jesus is someone who loves everybody," the man replied.

That did not make sense to Robert. No one loved him. No one had ever told him, "I love you, Robert." Why did Jesus love everyone but not him?

He thanked the man then left the church, confused about Jesus. However, two seeds were sown in his spirit that day. Firstly, he had become aware that Jesus was a man, not just a swear-word like all the others he heard. Secondly, he was aware of the power of images. There were no picture books in the Hicks house. Now he had seen the paintings in the church, Robert immediately understood the power of images. It was something he tucked away that day in his subconsciousness; it would be thirty years later that he'd retrieve that memory when he entered the world of publishing.

Early influences

The misery of life at No. 335 continued. The Hicks children knew it was best to keep out of their mother's way. She sometimes had a quick temper which could turn on them in an instant. She had never adapted to country life. She missed the pubs, nightlife and her friends in Birmingham. While her husband was in the army, she had a number of affairs with other men. It was at times like this she could be very clever using her children as an alibi or to disguise her true feelings.

Robert explains: "One morning, mother called me in from the garden. She said we were going on a trip to a place called Belle Vue in Manchester which was a zoological gardens. In a normal family, that is a regular event. In my family, it was like being told you are going on a trip to the moon.

"At the bus station, her reasons became clear. There she met her boyfriend. He was a black man and married, although his wife and children were overseas. This relationship would eventually lead to mother deserting her family and create a living hell for her children. As soon as she met him, mother abandoned me, making me sit in the seat behind them. I spent the day following them around the park. It's not right that a young boy should watch his mother kissing and snuggling up to her boyfriend. On the way home, mother ordered me to stay quiet about the trip, or face the consequences."

Because mother's boyfriend was a black man, and Robert was only eleven at the time, for the next twenty years, Robert would have only negative feelings towards black people. He somehow blamed them for his mother's desertion. Thankfully, he abandoned those feelings a long time ago—another way in which the Lord has rescued him.

"There were other times when she called me to sit on her lap. My mother did not hug or kiss or sit any of her children on her lap, except when an officer from the social work department was visiting. Mother wanted to prove she was a good parent in order to continue receiving her large family allowance. She stroked my hair and cuddled me during the interview then pushed me aside once it was over. I felt physically sick."

Winifred and William Hicks failed to exercise even the most basic parental duties. Doctors' visits were non-existent, so easily identifiable medical complaints which affected their children in later life—in Robert's case until he was fifteen—went unattended. Jean and Bernard both had severe squints. Bernard and Brian had speech problems. Bernard and John suffered from asthma.

Robert adds: "All our complaints could have been diagnosed and treated early and for free, certainly not as expensive as the clothes in mother's wardrobe. That's what would have happened in a normal family, but ours was far from normal."

Away from No. 335, Robert and his siblings did manage to encounter some normal people who offered respite from the sordid and corrupt life he knew with his own parents. A few doors down lived a family with two children and a lodger. The husband was tall and his wife looked at least ten years younger than him. Robert and his brothers regularly went round houses asking for empty lemonade and bleach bottles which they could take back to the village shop and exchange for sweets or a penny. This family was very poor so Robert knew they kept the bottles for themselves. Nonetheless, the wife would invite the children into the house for a friendly chat which the youngsters enjoyed.

He says: "These people made a huge impression on me. They confirmed there was more to life than the wanton abandonment we suffered at home."

Someone else who impressed was a kindly farmer who owned a large apple orchard. Children regularly climbed into the orchard to steal apples. One afternoon Robert, Bernard and Brian were helping themselves when the farmer came out. In their desperate bid to escape, Brian's trousers got caught in a branch and he left most of them behind as he jumped down. The following day, the farmer arrived at No. 335 to speak to the boys' parents but William was still in the army while Winifred was, as usual, in town.

"You stole my apples," the farmer said to Robert, Bernard and Brian standing innocently at the door.

"Not us," all three chimed.

"Yes, you did. I saw you," replied the farmer before clipping each round the ear. Then he added: "In future, if you want apples, come to the house and knock. I'll give you some. But don't climb the trees as you could do a lot of damage. OK?"

The brothers were amazed. The farmer was strict but fair. He had administered a punishment and their ears hurt for a second or two, but it was different from the prolonged and furious beatings they received from their father. Now their crime was forgotten and the boys could get all the apples they wanted.

"The farmer was a happy man who understood children," explains Robert. "Many years later, I realised his attitude was very much a biblical one with regard to forgiveness. When we confess our sin to God, he takes it and wipes it off his records. It no longer exists. I don't know if that farmer was a Christian. Perhaps he wasn't, which makes it all the more tragic that Christians go through life bearing grudges against others. Hand it over to the Lord and forgive."

A soldier of the cross

Robert recalls one more remarkable incident which showed that real love and tenderness did in fact exist in the world. He had been out playing alone with an old sword made from two pieces of wood, using it to chop off the heads of dandelions that had gone to seed. As he struck at the remnants, a stranger dressed in black appeared.

"He was small, had a small beard and looked very old. I'd seen travellers on the road but this man was different," says Robert. "He said hello then inquired what I had in my hand. He asked to see it so I handed it over. He held my sword up to the sky and suddenly I realised it looked like the cross I had seen in the old church. Then he said 'It is the sword of the cross, and you will be a soldier of the cross.'

"He put his hand on my head, blessed me then walked on. I stood looking at my sword for a moment then turned to look at the man. He had gone, vanished. I had heard of angels and I wondered if the man was one. There are verses in the Bible that speak of angels. They are ministering spirits (see Hebrews 1:14). When I look back at my childhood, I wonder if an angel was protecting me time and time again. God's angels are surrounding us and protecting us and, sometimes, they may even be seen."

Robert certainly needed protection from the chaotic household in which he lived. It was about to explode into even more madness and cruelty. One day his mother called her six children into the living room to make an announcement. She looked at them as one then said: "Your father's coming home tomorrow."

The intensity of the deprivation at home would have been unbearable if not for outside relief such as school or a few kindly neighbours. Robert's main reprieve consisted in his long walks through the fields and his humming (which acted as a pressure cooker to relieve the madness of daily family life).

Heaven and Hell

The pathetic row of children quivered half-naked, fear stamped on their faces. Some wore only a dirty vest, others had on nothing but pyjama bottoms. They had been dragged from their bed at midnight then kicked and punched into the kitchen, tumbling over each other while crying hysterically. They knew the drill: get in line; stand as quietly as possible; answer every question; never lie. Their father who had pulled them from their beds was drunk and screaming threats. He smashed one fist onto a table, while his other hand smacked loudly and randomly against the tender flesh of a child's leg or body, but never the face, as the resulting bruise might be seen by teachers or social workers.

William Hicks fired questions at his children, their submissive faces covered in a mixture of tears, saliva and blood.

"Where is your mother?" he screamed at the sorry little group. "Is she out with that black man again? Did she say where she was staying tonight?"

The children shook with terror. Their mother had left that afternoon to go into Birmingham. Recently, she had been doing this more often. She said she was working to get extra money and, because she finished late, would be staying with a friend or at her mother's house. What she did with the extra money was a mystery to her children. That day, Robert had to beg her to buy food before she left as there was nothing in the house for the six of them to eat, but she claimed she had no money. When she opened her purse to give him a few pennies for milk and bread, her son saw folded notes.

William Hicks had returned from the pub to find his wife gone and children in bed. Whisky fuelled his fury; he turned on all the house lights, waking his terrified children with screams and accusations. Seething, he raised his hand again, smacking someone's ear or another's bottom, demanding answers about their mother.

"Don't make me get my belt," he yelled.

It was the threat of violence, as much as the punches themselves, which caused terror. The little line of human misery before him quivered like a flimsy structure in an earthquake. The children dreaded their father's old army belt with its hard strap and huge buckle which could rip their flesh with one stroke.

William tried a different approach: "If you tell me where she is, I won't hurt you," he whispered.

Robert's eyes welled with tears as panic shot across his face. Tongue-tied, he struggled to make a plea for mercy.

"Dease, dad, don't hit dus. We don't know dwhere mum is," he whimpered.

William stood back, rage screaming from his eyes: "Liar, liar. She's with him, her boyfriend. You know where they are. Why won't you tell me?"

Arms raised, he flayed the army belt around their heads and the children raced to different hiding places to escape its searing cut. One went behind a chair, another squeezed between the cooker and the wall. Robert rushed to the small space near the gas meter. Eventually, their father would tire before collapsing into a stupor on the couch. Weeping quietly, the children returned to bed where they linked their bruised limbs in a protective huddle; that made it more difficult for their father to drag them out again should he wake before morning.

"These nightly interrogations filled us with terror. We lived with the threat of indiscriminate violence every day. It was painful being struck by father's belt, but the threat of it was enough to send us scattering. He would tease us like an animal teases its prey. That was the real cruelty," explains Robert.

The return of their father had initially been a source of excitement for the Hicks children. It also united them as they had spent so many years in different care homes and schools; they were like strangers to each other. A father was a point of reference. Robert was closest to his two younger brothers, Bernard and Brian. Jean was above Robert, and it was she whom he missed most whenever they were farmed out to institutions. She was gentle, funny, intelligent and motherly. The next oldest was John, sometimes called Jack, whose handsome looks charmed all the girls at school, followed by Donald, the step-brother, who, like Robert, was well built and a fearless fighter.

For a few hours on the day William Hicks arrived home, the children felt they had a proper father. When he walked through the door, he looked handsome in his huge grey coat, polished shoes and pressed trousers, held up by a large belt with a shiny buckle. For that brief interval before a kind of hell was unleashed, the children marvelled at their father's stories of bravery and courage. Even their mother seemed to smile more. "Could this be the start of a normal family?" wondered Robert.

"My father had helped liberate the inmates of a concentration camp," he says. "After witnessing such evil visited by human beings upon other human beings, I wondered how he could behave so brutally to his own children. That first day home, he acted like a real dad and a proper man. He laughed and joked and thrilled us with stories. But it was just an act. What was it in his character that made him violent and pitiless? He took a perverse please in beating, ridiculing and ignoring us. Father's sexual appetites, like mother's, were boundless. They were both self-centred and greedy individuals who seemed unable to relate to anyone else, especially their own children. What reasons could explain the way they behaved? I could not understand."

William brought an army friend with him who planned to stay a few days until he could make other arrangements. His visit only lasted one night. After the children were asleep, Winifred was confronted on the landing by two naked men—her husband and his friend. William wanted her to sleep with the man but she refused. Instead, he made her have sex with him while the other man stayed in the room. Years later, Robert's mother claimed she had been assaulted by her husband and several of his friends.

In the morning, the other man left after Winifred threatened to contact the police. She and her husband had a blazing row, the first of many stormy rows that turned life at No. 335 Stonehouse Lane into a war zone. The innocent casualties were six small children all under ten years of age.

Occasional relief

The intensity of the deprivation at home would have been unbearable if not for outside relief such as school or a few kindly neighbours. Robert's main reprieve consisted in his long walks through the fields and his humming. One day he bumped into a neighbour, Mr Taylor, who paid him a penny to fetch buckets of manure for his garden from the field where the horses grazed. When Robert's father heard of his son's endeavours, he demanded the same, but without any payment of course. Robert devised a cunning plan, an early sign of his shrewd business mind which would flourish later in his life.

"I part filled the bucket with straw so father only got half as much as Mr Taylor," he smiles. "If he had just said, 'Thank you' once, or rewarded me with a smile, that would have been the best payment ever. But he just grunted. He treated all his children like slaves who were there at his whim.

"I used to take Bernard and Brian to the cinema with the money Mr Taylor gave me. The Saturday matinée was one half-penny. We loved cowboy films like 'Hop-along Cassidy' and would act out the scenes on our way home. Of course, no one ever seemed to get hurt in his films. Hop-along managed to round all the bad guys up and take them off to jail after a punch-up or brief shootout. As children, we had no difficulty separating the pretend violence we saw on screen from the raw beatings we endured at home."

Despite the constant beatings they suffered and lack of basic possessions like clothes and toys, the Hicks children were remarkably moral. They did not randomly steal. Like most youngsters of the time, they sometimes lifted a bottle of milk from a doorstep on the way to school or snatched an apple from the greengrocer, but that was because they rarely had breakfast at home—except for lard on stale bread.

Robert recalls how nudity was common in the house, especially among the boys who regularly slept five to a bed. But this was mainly because of a lack of clothes and there was an innocence about it. The children wore the clothes they received from the care homes every day until they wore out. Then they had to beg and plead with their parents for replacements. Jean insisted her brothers knock before entering her bedroom and she never walked around the house without being properly dressed. In the slums, daily language was peppered with coarse, loud, aggressive swearing. Despite all this, Robert remembers his embarrassment at being naked for the first time in front of a stranger, a care worker.

"When I was about twelve, I was sent to a place called Middlemore Homes. The young man in charge of new arrivals told me I needed a haircut and shower. He made me undress and my clothes were put in a bag. I could tell from his disgusted look they must have been vile. I never saw any of those clothes again.

"After cutting my hair he ordered me to get in the shower. A large dollop of disinfectant was poured on my head and ran down my body like black tram lines. The care worker rubbed it into my scalp. This was the first time I was aware of being naked before another person and I was very embarrassed. The man's girlfriend arrived while I was in the shower, adding to my discomfort. She was very beautiful with a lovely smile. It seemed they were going on a date once he had finished with me."

As he grew older, Robert's conscience was challenged. He knew it was wrong to steal although he did once from a shop where he held a trusted position; he justified his action, but this reasoning did not sit well with him.

"One of the graces of God is that he places a sense of guilt within us, not to hound us, but so we are aware of right and wrong. I can remember from a very young age identifying those two absolutes. I had a sensitive conscience even before I became a Christian. Whenever I did something wrong, I tried to justify it, but I never felt comfortable. I knew my parents could tell the difference between right and wrong too. They just chose what was wrong: it's not that they were ignorant.

"Sometimes we stole because we were so desperate. But Jean was different. When she was thirteen, she ran away after dad had abused her. She spent the night cowering under a hedge. In the morning, she actually knocked on someone's door asking for a glass of water. Can

"Today, I pulled some of the farmer's carrots out of the ground to eat. I put the green tops back into the soil but I don't think they will grow again. I hope he won't mind me taking the carrots as I was so hungry."

you imagine this terrified, abused and starving girl standing on a doorstep, politely asking for some water? She knew it was wrong to steal the milk on their doorstep, even though she had been freezing in a hedge all night, beaten, abused and thirsty. My sister is my hero.

"On paper, the Hicks children were a bunch of juvenile delinquents. We all ran away from home numerous times. We became well known to the police who had the task of taking us home, sometimes after a night in the cells. Of course, mother and father would put on an act of concerned parents while talking to the officer at the door. Once he left, we were soundly beaten. In the police notebooks, we were the criminals, but the crimes from which we were trying to escape were never detected."

He adds: "Why did we not tell someone? Why did we not report what was happening at No. 335? In today's world, child abuse is high on society's agenda, but back in the 1940s, the nation was recovering from a world war. People's attitudes to what went on behind closed doors were different. Besides, most households in the slums were places of abuse, whether of wives or children, and sometimes husbands. To the world, we were just more walking wounded, another anonymous family in a long line of refugees hobbling along the road; why should we be singled out more than anyone else?"

At school

Schooling for the Hicks children was a haphazard affair. This was partly due to the fact they were in and out of care homes, and partly because their parents could not be bothered to register them. In the end, they were sent to the local primary school as it gave their mother more free time for herself. Robert's speech impediment meant he was labelled as retarded. No one thought to examine his intelligence or send him for a proper medical examination. None of the teaching staff believed his problem was physical; it was immediately labelled a mental defect. Over the years, Robert learnt to use his throat muscles to make sounds he was unable to make with his tongue because it was attached to the floor of his mouth. But teachers believed he was just lazy or stupid or both, so he was written off.

"In defence of the teachers, I would have to point out the average size class at this time was around sixty," explains Robert. "I suppose there simply wasn't time to give any child one-to-one attention. It was post-war, and there was a lack of staff and resources."

Inside, he was a young intelligent boy, with a drive and eagerness to learn but receiving no direction or guidance. Being sidelined by the education authorities meant he had difficulty reading or writing. By the age of ten, he was well behind his peers. He had trouble seeing words or writing them clearly and it wasn't until many years later that he was discovered to be dyslexic. One night, Robert was watching a programme with Esther Rantzen who was interviewing actress Susan Hampshire and former racing driver, Jackie Stewart, who were both dyslexic. Listening to them talk about the difficulties they had experienced at school and in adulthood, Robert suddenly realised, he, too, suffered from the condition.

Yet, school was not a complete educational no-man's land. Robert had a very active and perceptive mind. He daydreamed a lot while developing his gift for reading people's characters. Whether teachers or other pupils, Robert could quickly discern their real personalities, their motives and their desires. It was a God-given gift which would serve him well in his future business career. And there was one subject at which he did excel—arithmetic. Amazingly, this ability got him into trouble with his maths teacher, Mr Woolley.

"He wrote some complicated sums on the blackboard and, to my amazement, I was able to see the answers straightaway without going through the process. It was like I was standing on a river bank and I could see the way across using stepping stones. My classmates, however, needed to go step by step very slowly and look back at where they had come from before proceeding.

"After five minutes, I'd done all the sums and put my hand up to say I was finished. Mr Woolley was amazed and accused me of cheating. He tried to make out I had copied the answers from a book on his desk while his back was turned. That would have been impossible, but he would just not accept I had completed the sums so quickly. In the end, he marched me down to the headmaster's office. Both men stood over me accusingly. They demanded a full confession as to how I had cheated. Mr Woolley was so angry, he wanted to cane me but I protested my innocence. I had done nothing wrong. Then the headmaster decided to give me a test right there in his office."

Robert panicked. Feeling under pressure, he wondered if he would make a mistake and be labelled a cheat. Had the first sums just been a fluke? He had no option but to do the impromptu test. To the amazement of both teachers, Robert got all the answers correct without the need to write anything down.

"That day, aged just thirteen, I made a real discovery about myself: I wasn't useless. I could actually do something. All my life I had been branded as stupid, unlovable, unneeded, unable to even talk, and now I had found something I could

"I am good at maths in school. I am always at the top of my class. The teacher said I am good enough to be top of the school. I can see the answers without a lot of thinking. Is it because I am thinking all the time? I like maths but I wish I could read as well. I can work out numbers easily but I cannot understand the alphabet. I don't know why."

do. I had a talent. I don't know who was more startled—me or Mr Woolley and the headmaster."

Such happy discoveries were all too brief in Robert's young life. The reality of the misery at 335 Stonehouse Lane consumed his waking and sleeping hours. William's drunken night interrogations of his children grew in intensity as his wife became increasingly absent. One night he ordered his children to stand naked for hours in the kitchen while he made all kinds of threats. Sometimes Winifred would spend days away, claiming she was working night shifts. William's concern was not her neglect of their children but her neglect of him and her desire to be with another man. The fact she chose a black man particularly infuriated her husband.

One day the children were huddled in their room, listening to their parents having a blazing row. Winifred was stronger mentally and could easily dominate her husband. But William had brute strength on his side and the fights often turned physical. The screams and sounds of punches and slaps echoed around the house. Still covering his ears, Robert heard his mother yelling: "Robert, get the police, your dad's killing me."

The youngster scampered to the public phone box in the village square. He knew how to dial 999 in an emergency. He asked the operator for the police.

A stern voice asked: "What's wrong, son? What's your address?"

"My dad is hittin' my mumb," he replied awkwardly.

"Your dad's hitting your mum? Where do you live?"

Robert took a deep breath: "Dree, dree five Donehouse Dane, Bartley Dween."

"Where? I can't understand you, son. Are you playing a joke? It's very serious to lie to the police."

"No, no. Ah cand dawk properwe. I dwiv at dree, dree five Donehouse Dane. Please comb."

After a few more attempts, the police managed to get the correct address. When they arrived, an officer lectured William about beating his wife. All the time, William glared at his son. As soon as the police left, Robert got a severe beating. He had crossed the line by incriminating his father.

He adds: "My father was a vengeful man who would make his son pay for this treachery many, many times."

Mother leaves

But it was Robert's mother who delivered the next devastating blow to her children. On the morning of June 9th, 1952, Winifred Hicks called her six children into the front room. She ordered them to hug her. The younger ones quickly obeyed this surprise command, but Robert, who was eleven, stood back. There was something odd about her request. Her tone was different. Then Winifred looked at her children and calmly announced she was leaving them to start a new life with another man. They would not see her again. The children began to cry hysterically, begging her to stay. Robert stood back.

"It was like a scene from a grotesque pantomime. Our mother was telling us that we must hug her for the last time. Can anyone imagine how we felt? I could not touch her so she came over and hugged me but I kept my hands at my side. I remember her smell, that same smell she had when she came at Christmas to fetch me from the Erdington Home and I felt sick.

"Mother calmly went upstairs to get her bags, ignoring her desperate children's pleas as she came down and walked to the door. There was pandemonium as weeping children implored their mother not to leave. She looked into their anguished eyes, ignoring the fear she saw, then she grew angry as the wailing and howling from her children grew louder; they placed their starved bodies between her and the door. She turned on them, accusing them of not loving her, of never having loved her, so she had no choice. But she did. She was abandoning her six children to go and live with the man I had seen her with that day on our trip. Mother would shortly give birth to his baby. She was choosing this man over us."

The No. 12 bus to Birmingham was pulling up at the stop opposite their house. Winifred boarded just as it was about to leave. Jack jumped on his bike, chasing the bus as it drove off. Brian ran alongside, banging on the window where his mother sat impassively, begging tearfully for her to get off. She stared straight ahead. Little asthmatic Jack peddled as fast as he could, but his lungs were failing and the bus picked up speed. As it disappeared into the distance, Jack hung over the bike's handlebars gasping for breath.

Soon, it was out of sight.

Robert stood impassively in the doorway while his siblings staggered around in the road, crying, bewildered, stunned and fearful. In a few hours, their father would be home from the pub.

Robert aged 17; he was destined to become a boy preacher.

19 A family adrift

The hot summer wind blew blissfully through Robert's hair as he climbed the grassy slope up to Frankley Beeches Reservoir. It was here that he learnt to pray.

This huge expanse of water near his house in Bartley Green served a large part of the city of Birmingham and still does today. Robert loved sitting by its side, following the sunlight dancing over its surface or a cloud's reflection caught in the still water. He marvelled how several miles away in one of Britain's biggest cities, people were washing themselves or their cars or making tea, flushing their toilets and producing goods in row after row of factories, unaware the water came from Frankley Beeches.

"Most people in Birmingham did not give a second thought to where the source of their water was, but I could sit and dangle my feet in its cool, priceless liquid," explains Robert. "Years later when I returned to this idyllic spot, a born-again Christian who loved and lived for the Lord, I realised this was where I first came to know him. As a young boy, still tongue-tied, abandoned by my mother and beaten regularly by my drunken father, I would sneak off to Frankley Beeches which became my open-air church.

"Psalm 19 begins, 'The heavens declare the glory of

"I know how to count the stars in the sky. I make a circle with my first finger and thumbs and stretch it from my eye until I can count a hundred stars. Then I move the circle around the sky and count how many circles it needs to cover the sky. There are hundreds and hundreds of stars."

God; and the firmament sheweth his handiwork.' Pagans who worship the earth are missing the point. They worship an object; Christians worship the One who created the object. If you are a child of creation, there is a sense in which the universe, the stars in the sky and the earth, even Frankley Beeches Reservoir, are all for you. They were put there by a loving Creator for us to enjoy and to reflect his majesty.

"Back in those days when I was barely a teenager, I, too, like the good citizens of my native city, was receiving life, spiritual and cleansing, from a source I was only dimly aware off. I knew about God but did not yet know him. But he knew me, little Robert Hicks, 335 Stonehouse Lane, Bartley Green, Birmingham, England. Like the woman in the Bible who met Jesus at the well, I too thirsted for the Water of Life and I was starting to drink."

In the days and months after Robert's mother walked out on her children, the Hicks house exploded into chaos. Robert's mother had left two dresses behind as well as the coat he and his brothers used to keep warm in bed. His father took them all into the kitchen where he cut them up with a knife. Robert watched his father stamping over the pieces, cursing and shouting. The youngster wondered why his father did not sell them or pawn them instead. Destroying them seemed wasteful.

Social Services descended to clear up a mess made by two parents who had never really accepted that title or its responsibility. Their neglected children were farmed out to care homes, often in different parts of the country, so that the fragile friendships they had formed while living under one roof were once again ripped apart.

At No. 335, unspeakable evil was beginning to take form. Jean ran away several times as she feared most what would happen in her mother's absence. Sometimes she was sent to the Erdington Home, sometimes to one of her relatives in Sheffield, Yorkshire. When she was returned to No. 335, she would immediately run away, often sleeping rough in the countryside or in Birmingham's dirty and dangerous back streets.

When they were at home, the children would stay out in the fields or hide in the coalhouse until their father fell asleep and it was safe for them to come in. Brian had his own hiding place in the loft and would not come down at night until the others assured him their father was in a deep sleep. There was rarely any food in the house and they had to beg him to give them money or to buy basic provisions. The late-night beatings and interrogations continued at will.

"One day I returned from the field to find Brian in agony," adds Robert. "Father had used a brass fender from the front of the fire to beat his leg black and blue. When I saw how badly swollen it was, I was shocked because it was an horrific beating, even for my father. I honestly thought Brian would lose his leg. When he limped into school the next day, he told the teachers he had fallen off his bike. I was terrified. I was also terrified I would be next as he had already picked fights with me, and he wasn't afraid to use his fists and feet when beating his children."

William hated an untidy house. He expected his children to cook and clean, make him tea on demand and iron his clothes. The slightest error such as tea that was too cold or a trouser crease in the side rather than at the front earned them a sharp beating. The children had accepted that their mother was not returning. Jack managed to track down the man she had gone to live with but when the youngster knocked on the door of the house, he was refused entry. The man claimed his mother was not there but, as he arrived, Jack had glimpsed her through the window. He shouted her name but she never came out, ignoring her son's pitiful pleas.

Abuse at home

The first time William raped his daughter was when she had just turned thirteen. Jean was growing into a beautiful young woman who, nonetheless, lacked self-confidence because of her severe squint which had never even been examined by an optician, let alone treated. The abuse started one night after Jean cooked a meal for her father.

"When he finished eating, the gas meter ran out and the lights went off. He said he had no money to put in so we were ordered to bed. That night, in the dark, cold kitchen, my father crudely raped my sister. My eyes fill with tears still when I remember this horror. It would not be the first time he would do it. In preparing notes for this book, I wondered whether I should omit these facts from the story, but having spoken to Jean, and with her permission, I decided to include them. Many people have suffered such abuse and they need to know there is hope and people who will help.

"Father would purge his conscience by singling Jean out for treats like a trip to the cinema or a new blouse. But he also told her if she revealed what he was doing, he would kill her. Jean had watched her drunken, violent father beat her mother often enough to know it was a promise he was capable of keeping.

"Early one morning I saw Jean leave father's bedroom. She said she'd been there all night but nothing more. Her personality began to change. My lovely, bright and funny sister became downcast and surly. We boys were all too young to understand what was happening. When Jean eventually told me, I could not take it in. Later in life, I became friends with the journalist and broadcaster, Esther Rantzen, who presented the BBC programme, 'That's Life'. Esther went on to found the charity 'ChildLine' and has done so much to make people aware of the reality of child abuse. Esther told me that even if I had challenged my father at the time, he may well have killed both Jean and me.

"I remember the afternoon when Jean suddenly blurted out she wanted to kill father and had come up with a plan. When he fell asleep, she would turn on the gas for the gas fire in his room, ensuring the windows were closed and gaps in the window blocked up with newspaper. We all laughed, thinking it was just a game. Someone joked we would have to make sure we had enough money for the meter to do the job properly. Jean frowned. It was then I realised she was serious—absolutely serious. The only thing that stopped her was father's habit of sleeping with one eye partly open. Jean was convinced he could see us and was too afraid of what he would do if she failed."

Jean confirmed she wanted this awful episode to be included in her brother's story. She says: "I realise now that I was not to blame for the terrible things my father did to me or the fear for my life he instilled in me. For many years, my life was so damaged that I occasionally considered suicide as the only possible escape. Of course, it would not have been.

"I do hope that Bobby's story will be read by many and that, in the process, children even today who are threatened by adults close to them might find genuine friends who can protect and save them from the many torments that we, as a family, had to endure."

Robert's own escape from the horrors at home was to spend more time out in the fields, humming constantly to himself. The beautiful countryside filled him with wonder, especially on clear winter nights when he would lie for hours, marvelling at the awning of stars in the frosty sky above. He knew there was something more than him, more than this world, but he had not yet found it, or at least given it a name. For the moment, it was enough to survive life at No. 335.

When he started reading and copying out his Bible to help form words after his operation, Robert rejoiced at the story of the Garden of Eden. The fields around Bartley Green had become an Eden for him. Here God was calling him in, not casting him out like Adam and Eve.

"It was here I learnt about the majesty of the Creator and how, even as a tongue-tied young boy, labelled retarded and useless, I could share in the divine composer's unending and utterly harmonious concerto which, in the poetic vision of the Psalmist, makes the stars sing and the trees skip," he explains.

Betty

The landscape at home was also about to take a dramatic change. Robert's father arrived one day with a woman called Betty. She was in her twenties, plump, and had a Welsh accent. Unknown to the children, she was a prostitute and she quickly settled into No. 335. The children were unsure how to respond to a woman other than their mother living at home with them. However, they discovered Betty had a lighter side to her character. She would hug them, ask how they were doing at school, and even prepared meals. Their mother had skulked silently around the house, rarely talking to her children except for a command to get to bed or when instructing them to pass on a message to their father that she would be gone for the night. Betty started to redecorate the living room, talking to Jean about what colours to use. The little girl finally had a friend and someone to take her father's attention away from her, and keep her out of his bed.

William had a habit of throwing his mail unopened

"I keep humming quietly to myself. I don't know why but the vibration from the humming stops the pain from thoughts I cannot share with anyone. I like thinking but I wish I could talk as well."

into a drawer. Apart from unpaid bills, most of it consisted of final demands for fines, not least to the courts. He was ordered to contribute towards Jean's stay at Erdington but he failed to make any payments.

Eventually, this casual disregard led to him receiving a court summons. Robert knew his father kept a jar filled with money below his bed which none of the children dared touch, no matter how hungry they were. It seemed William had decided to call the court's bluff, hoping to pay a large fine at the last moment, but the judge did not allow him the opportunity. He immediately sentenced the neglectful father to forty days in jail.

Betty announced the news to the children, promising to stay on in their father's absence. They were delighted this caring woman they had come to cherish would be their guardian, and that they would not have to be split up once again and sent to various care homes. As the weeks passed, Robert noticed the money in his father's jar seemed to be getting less, but he never raised it with Betty. He was just relieved to have a real mother figure in the house, someone who allowed him to cuddle up to her and who stroked his hair.

He says: "I did not know how to respond to this physical attention, not least because my mother never touched or caressed me at all. Although, by this time, I was aware of the differences between boys and girls, I suppose I was a late developer. I am so glad, as it proved to be my preservation, praise God. When Betty's caressing became more intense, I pretended to be asleep. I was just delighted to be living in a quiet, calm house with a gentle, mother figure in charge. Sex was the last thing on my mind."

It wasn't long before this family atmosphere started to break down. Soon the money jar was empty. Betty's plans to decorate were put on hold and she began to be more absent. One day she came home with a sailor who had one leg in a plaster cast. They spent a lot of time locked in father's room. A few days later, another man from the services, a soldier with a cast on his arm, walked in with Betty.

"In our ignorance, we regarded Betty as a sort of Florence Nightingale figure, caring for injured servicemen at our home. It seemed such a loving thing to do, we were even proud of her," explains Robert.

"More and more men were coming to our house. The neighbours were talking about us, very loudly. I began to realise something was not right. In the slums, neighbours had accused mother of running a brothel while father was in the army. Now it seemed history was repeating itself.

"One evening, Betty dressed Jean up, put makeup on her and took her into Birmingham. Late at night, my sister returned alone. She said Betty had gone off with some men and would not be coming back. Jean had no choice but to start walking the twelve miles home alone to Bartley Green. Two men stopped her, asked why she was out on her own so late then put her on the last bus home, paying her fare. I believe they were guardian angels dispatched to look after a vulnerable young girl and keep her from harm.

"We didn't understand what was happening but we were sad that this friendly, caring woman had abandoned us just like our mother had. Mother's rejection of us was an evil act but somehow I did not miss her. When Betty left, there was a void in my life that was difficult to fill.

"As long as Betty was around, father was less violent. During her brief stay, Betty came to symbolise everything I needed from a mother. Her departure opened old wounds. Once again, I felt betrayed, alone, helpless and stupid. Betty had gone somewhere; I was going nowhere, except back to a care home.

"For Jean, there were other fears. Father turned his attentions to her once more. He would come home around 2am, drunk, having taken the bus from Birmingham for part of the journey, then walking the rest. He would shout at Jean to get up and make him something to eat. From the age of thirteen to fifteen, he raped and abused her. Jean tried to kill herself several times. On one attempt, she swallowed a handful of pills and was rushed to hospital. The doctors questioned her motives, but, with father sitting at the side of the bed, Jean was unable to tell the truth. However, that near discovery frightened him. He was terrified of his secret coming out so he never abused Jean again, at least not physically."

It all comes to a head

The next few years at Bartley Green passed in the same stale manner. The Hicks children were in and out of care homes, only meeting fleetingly at No. 335. When they did, their conversation stumbled with the awkwardness of strangers. William had a job working in a factory. He spent even longer in the pub after work, bemoaning his life, his wife and getting drunk. Little money came into the house. Robert and his siblings relied on free school dinners for food and care homes for clothes. At school, they ate any food put before them, even those things they did not like. They had learnt it was better to have a full stomach of horrible food, than a stomach empty of anything. Birthdays and Christmas went unmarked, just more cold days in a house devoid of love or affection. By 1956, Robert, now aged fifteen, was the only one of the six still living at home. He alone suffered the regular beatings with a weary acceptance, curling up in a ball when his father's screaming accusations stopped and seconds later, his fists and feet would rain a relentless bout of punching and kicking. Robert offered his back as a target, while protecting his head. When it finished, the teenager picked himself up from the floor, checked his ribs and bones for fractures, then quietly hummed to himself as he limped through the door to his beloved fields where he remained as his father fell asleep.

There was no hint one particular evening that Robert's life and his relationship with his father would come to a head. That afternoon after school, he had cleaned and polished the front room, the one in which social workers sat during their inspection visits. This cunning tactic, introduced by his father, fooled visitors into believing this was the house of a man doing his best to raise a family singlehandedly, and worthy of a large family allowance. Upstairs, Robert's room was bare and shabby. The deception made Robert sick but he dared not say anything or he would be beaten.

As usual, he was asleep in bed when he was roused by the sound of his father thumping on the front door before managing to fit his key in the lock. He was drunk so he would be hungry. Robert's only hope was he would be so drunk he would fall asleep in a chair before he could command his son to come down and make him something to eat. Robert listened to his father downstairs shouting angry accusations at his shadow. Then he heard the order he dreaded: "Bobby, get down here and make me a bacon sandwich. I know you're not sleeping. Hurry up."

He entered the kitchen which was warm from the cooker. Every time his father left the house, the gas would run out, yet as soon as he returned, he always had money to warm himself up. Robert cooked the bacon then made tea, remembering to pour the milk into the jam jar first to avoid the hot tea cracking the glass. His father offered him a bacon sandwich, but his son had learnt it was unwise to deprive him of his food and he quietly declined it.

This was how it always began. The fumbling of the lock; the demand for food; silence as his father chewed, drunk and angry. The storm was simmering and about to erupt. The next stage was a ranting monologue.

"You know Donald isn't mine," said William with a sneer. "Nor was Brian or the girl your mother gave away. I was in the army and she was getting pregnant by someone else. That's the sort of woman you called 'mother'."

William gulped his tea. Robert waited for the next seething rant to begin. Still chewing, his father went on: "Have you seen your mother? You know where she is don't you? You were the one who called the police. Remember, Bobby? Why did you do that? She was pregnant by a black man and you called the police on me. You knew she had done wrong yet you betrayed me, too."

Robert picked at his shirt. Ironically, the bright yellow shirt he was wearing was the only thing he could ever remember his father buying him. He had got it from a man he knew in the pub and Robert loved it.

"I bought you that shirt, Bobby," said his father accusingly. "What did she ever buy you? Nothing, that's what."

Another frightening silence followed as William lamented his life. It was the warning sign Robert was waiting for. He moved to the other side of the kitchen, preparing himself for the flurry of blows that would shriek down on him like warplanes diving to unlock their bombs. Then something inside him snapped. He realised this was his moment—now or never. He had anticipated this moment for years, imagining it in his dreams. He had practised punches and moves alone in the fields. The boy called useless, unloved and unwanted was ready to fight for freedom.

Before him stood a monster, not his father. He had never been that. Robert was not his son, just a stranger on whom he would shortly vent his wrath. His mind was in turmoil; Robert tightened his fist, checking his father's movement out of the corner of his eye. Yet something in Robert baulked at his plan. It was not natural for a child to hit a parent.

His thoughts were interrupted as, in a flash, William leapt at his son, his face contorted in fury. Robert turned to meet the attack, sinking his fist into his father's belly. Winded, William crumpled to his knees, a look of utter bewilderment on his face. Robert aimed his knee at his father's chin, catching it full on. Blood and some teeth hurled from his father's mouth. As he fell back, William bit his lip, splattering blood onto Robert's yellow shirt.

"At that moment, just before my knee connected with his chin, I saw into my father's soul," says Robert. "I saw the same fear in his eyes that he had seen in ours every time he thrashed us with his belt or his fists or his large heavy boots. I knew that I had won. The evil spell he had held over me for all these years was broken. For the first time in my young life, I was free."

In that same moment, Robert caught sight of the bread knife on the kitchen table. It would have been so easy. But there was no need. The battle was over. The beast was defeated and Robert claimed victory.

He turned and walked out of the kitchen. His father's blood was already drying on his bright yellow shirt.

Robert (extreme left) at work.

Free at last

The shop manageress put down her book, gently encouraging Robert to try and say the word once more. Mrs Siddall, a former nurse, had taken an instant liking to the teenager since he had started his employment as an errand boy a few weeks earlier. Robert was a conscientious worker who got on well with customers. It was obvious he had a number of social problems, not least his ability to pronounce his words clearly. His personal hygiene was also suspect, which probably owed much to the fact he wore the same shirt and jumper to work every day. Some of the elderly ladies who came to the store found it difficult to understand what the new boy was saying, although he was very polite and helpful.

Mrs Siddall was divorced with grown-up daughters of her own. She was training as a manageress at one of Birmingham's oldest grocery stores, George Mason's, and wanted to help Robert improve his speech. The shop closed every day for a lunch hour and, during that time, she gave the teenager some simple spelling tests. But his efforts to say the words out loud ended in frustration, baffling the mother-of-two. Observing Robert at work, Mrs Siddall knew he was intelligent, but was puzzled why he could not pronounce his words more clearly.

"Robert, let me have a look in your mouth," she commanded as someone used to telling patients what she wanted them to do.

Robert stood awkwardly, opening his mouth as wide as he could. He was embarrassed as his boss took hold of his face and peered into his gaping mouth.

"My goodness," she exclaimed. "I can see what your problem is straightaway. You're tongue-tied, Robert, and quite badly at that.

I've never known anyone your age to be like this. It's something doctors usually pick up in babies. Did your mother never take you to see a doctor?"

Robert could not tell her that doctors' visits were never high on his parents' agenda. He had never heard the phrase "tongue-tied". He was just glad to hear someone give a name to what was preventing him from speaking. Within two weeks, Robert had an appointment at Selly Oak Hospital as a day patient, on his one afternoon off from George Mason's. This hospital is now the main military hospital for troops returning from Afghanistan.

The youngster lay on a bed in preparation for his operation when the doctor entered followed by a posse of medical students. Each took a turn to stare into Robert's mouth then made notes on their clipboards while shaking their heads.

"I felt like a specimen in the lab," recounts Robert. "The doctor asked me to recite the alphabet so the students could hear my poor pronunciation. However, at fifteen, I did not know the alphabet. I got as far as the letter 'd' then he had to help me. It was humiliating.

"The students took turns to examine me like I wasn't even human. I was then taken to theatre where the doctor froze my tongue and, moments later, simply snipped the two pieces of membrane on either side which had pinned it to the floor of my mouth. It was as easy as that. I was free. I could talk like anyone else. I felt like a prisoner who had been wrongly convicted, finally let out of his cell, desperate to tell his story. All my young life, my outward appearance made the

> "I dreamed again of the red robin that I trapped in a cage. I now understand why he kept hurting himself trying to escape from the trap. I now understand why he escaped and never came back. One day I will escape. One day I will be free."

world dismiss me as stupid and backward. My clothes were dirty rags. I was usually too embarrassed to speak and, when I did, I sounded clumsy, like a baby. Inside, my mind was buzzing and observant. I had so many questions and was keen to learn.

"After the operation as I waited in the outpatients department, a growing anger towards my parents intensified. I reflected how the operation had taken only minutes. I was going home that same afternoon. If mother or father had bothered to take notice of their children, they could have saved me years of misery, pain and exclusion.

"They could have fixed Jean and Brian's squints; Jack and Bernard's asthma could have been treated and my speech corrected while I was still an infant. My father had not even come to Selly Oak with me that day. Our parents had never been proper parents; they had been our jailers."

"Read out loud and write down the words"

William Hicks turned quickly when he heard his son open the door of No. 335. He didn't ask about the operation or how Robert felt or if he had a follow-up appointment with the local GP. He only wanted to know if he had received his wages so he could head off to the pub. In those days, the teenager earned the equivalent of £2.26 a week. His father took most of it, leaving him one shilling and one penny, or 5p, to pay for food, bus fares and clothes.

Since the fight, William no longer physically attacked his son. However, the psychological bullying continued. His father denounced Robert as a burden who had stayed on too long at school, sponging off his father for food and rent. He was told to get a job and start contributing to the house upkeep, which effectively meant his father's pockets. His room remained bare and dirty; the kitchen was barren of food; and the whole house froze when the gas ran out, which was frequently. William may have long ago left Birmingham's slums, but he retained a slum mentality so that No. 335 was just a slum in the country. Downstairs, the main lounge remained spotless.

There was a sigh of relief from his teachers when Robert confirmed he was leaving school. It was as if they were delighted to see another difficult pupil walk out the main gate. At fifteen, Robert was barely able to read and write, but his mathematical skills remained an untapped resource and his dyslexia was undiagnosed. The awkward, inarticulate boy, who was entertained rather than educated in class, had never been earmarked as university material; he was just more truculent factory fodder. Robert recalls the coldness of his departure. "The teacher bent down, looked me in the eye then whispered in my ear, 'What a waste.' I vowed, at that moment, I would prove him wrong. I would make something of my life and be successful. I did not waste my time at school: I never got a chance."

As he lay in bed that night, the surgeon's advice rang fresh in Robert's ears: "Read a book out loud while writing the words," he said. "That way, you can start learning how to use your tongue so your speech will gradually improve. You must read a book, Robert, the largest book you can find."

It seemed an impossible task. The only printable materials in Stonehouse Lane were the Family Allowance books and the Daily Mirror. It was Robert's job most mornings to fetch the newspaper from the nearest newsagent, which meant a two-mile round trip

"The way for me to overcome not being able to read is page by page and word by word even if it takes years to do it."

before he walked the same distance to school, or earn a severe beating from his father. As a result, he was regularly late for class registration, the perfect excuse for teachers to scold him as lazy.

The day after his operation, Robert was back at work. Mrs Siddall lovingly fussed over him, anxious for every detail of the hospital visit and his prognosis. He told of the doctor's advice and how he had found a large book at home along with an ancient ink pen which was essentially a wooden handle with a metal nib pushed in at one end. All he needed now was ink, a lot of ink, because the book called The Holy Bible contained 1,400 pages, with no pictures. Mrs Siddall put her hand to her mouth in excitement. She fetched a huge tin of industrial ink which she had bought for him. Robert was humbled and delighted. It was big enough to fill hundreds of desk ink wells. He beamed as he accepted this precious gift.

Cycling to George Mason's that morning, Robert's mouth was still very tender and raw where the surgeon had operated, but he had been practicing his "T" sound, which previously had always been voiced as a "D". For example, the word "they" came out as "dey" and "there" was heard as "dere". He felt incredibly humble as Mrs Siddall congratulated his efforts and then handed over the huge tin of ink. He was unused to such kindness and it overwhelmed him. Robert's home life had been the very negation of selflessness and generosity. There were one or two people in the care homes who had treated him kindly. But human warmth, in the shape of a gentle hug or a comforting smile, was foreign to the teenager. For the first time in his life, partly because of his operation and partly because someone had shown him unconditional kindness, Robert Hicks was finally able to say: "Thank you."

Before he left the shop, one more miracle took place. Robert explains: "I knew we had no paper at home. Ours was not a house where children's colourful paintings adorned the fridge or kitchen wall. Our family's stains were there for all to see, if only someone had looked.

"That week, George Mason's was being monitored by a man from a company which checked our stock sales record, most popular items and so on. The man had sheets of used spreadsheet paper and he was making notes on the blank side. I told him about my plans to copy out a book and I was amazed when he gave me a huge bundle, saying I could have more if I wanted. It took me several days to transport all the paper home in the basket of the bike I used for deliveries."

The Holy Bible book

From the day after his operation, Robert's nightly routine followed the same pattern. After work, he would come home and start to copy out his book immediately. When his father came home, Robert hoped he would be too drunk to demand food and that he would fall straight into bed.

When only his father's snoring broke the silence, the teenager knew it was safe to get his paper, ink and Holy Bible book from the small space behind the gas meter where he kept it hidden.

Robert's night-time occupation was unknown to his father; he feared the Holy Bible book would be ripped apart or thrown into the garbage. Alone in the dark, with only a candle providing light, he placed the valuable items on the wooden box which covered the gas meter, facing a cold, brick wall. There, until the early hours, he would write and speak the words aloud with such joy and purpose, he often found it difficult to stop

Although his aim in copying out this unknown book was solely to improve his speech, Robert slowly realised it was having a strange effect on him. He began to take in what he was reading. The Holy

Bible book was divided into two main sections, The Old Testament and The New Testament, and each of these consisted of smaller books with a different name. The first book in the Old Testament was called Genesis. When Robert read how God created the heavens and the earth and the earth was "without form and void", that phrase struck him because it echoed his own family life. He knew what a void was; it was the empty, fractured life he had lived, traded between parents who shunned him, and care homes where he was just one more abandoned child. He wondered if the God mentioned in Genesis and whose Spirit hovered over the water, could hover over the Hicks family one day and give it form?

When he read about the Garden of Eden, Robert thought of the lush fields surrounding Bartley Green and Frankley Beeches Reservoir. He could understand God creating something so beautiful. But why, if God loved the world, had the world just been involved in a terrible war with bombs and shells tearing cities and the countryside apart? If God loved everyone, why did children like him suffer when they had done nothing wrong?

Writing out the Holy Bible book left Robert puzzled, questioning and enlightened. He loved the poetic language, often marvelling how the author, someone probably called King James, could write so beautifully. He worked his way through several of the books in the Old Testament then switched to the New Testament. There he encountered the man named Jesus whose painting he had seen many years ago in the little church. He loved reading about Jesus and his parables. Robert remembered how he had asked the vicar: "Who is this Jesus?" Now, he was beginning to know him and he seemed unlike anyone else Robert had ever met.

Some phrases and passages affected him so profoundly; like huge boulders they stopped him in his tracks. What did it mean to become a new creature in Christ Jesus? Could that happen to anyone? And if

Jesus' Heavenly Father was so powerful and good, could he not sort out Robert's drunken, abusive, violent earthly father, sleeping in the next room? One thing was certain: Robert loved reading this book. One afternoon, Jack tried to persuade his brother to go into town, something Robert enjoyed. However, he could not bear being away from his writing, using up every spare minute he had.

"There I was, a boy of fifteen, barely able to read or write and with absolutely no theological training whatsoever," says Robert. "I knew nothing about terms such as the Trinity or the Incarnation. But I would read something Jesus said then stop and reflect on it. This meditation brought the Bible alive. What did Jesus mean about living a life of love and having a personal relationship with him? I was aware my speech was improving from all my reading, but something else was also growing inside me, something I could not yet put into words.

"The Holy Spirit was doing a work in me. The Bible is not just a book. It is alive, the living Word in pen and paper. The Bible was becoming my teacher, my literature, my friend, but above all, my salvation. It is the manual for life. It is the complete book." He adds: "This startling revelation at such a young age planted a seed in my life so that many years later, as a publisher, I vowed that I would get a free copy of the Bible, New Testament or Gospels into the hands of as many people as possible, all over the world. Little did I know then that tens of millions of people would receive a copy—and one day at Buckingham Palace, I would hand one to the Queen through her office."

What is your religion, boy?

As he continued to write out the Bible, Robert felt a desire to attend church. He remembered his time at Middlemore Care Home when all children entering the institution had their personal information collected with military precision. The same questions were repeated with weary familiarity. They were asked their name, address and father's occupation, in addition to their school year and whether they had any medication to take. The more experienced youngsters had their replies remembered by heart, although the first time the questions were addressed to Robert, one left him stumped.

"What is your religion?" inquired the receptionist at the young boy standing before her in his new clean underwear that had been supplied by the social work department. She had been warned this twelve-year-old boy was retarded, still unable to speak. All the youngsters had been washed, checked for lice and given new clothes in exchange for the foul-smelling rags which were already in the incinerator. She only required an answer to one simple question, and then he could be passed through to the dormitory.

"Can you tell me your religion?" she asked again, very deliberately. "Are you Church of England?"

Robert felt that church sounded far too important for someone like him from the slums. He shook his head.

The woman attempted some more suggestions: "Roman Catholic? Baptist?"

The names meant nothing to Robert. Finally, the frustrated receptionist cried: "You can be Methodist. We'll put you down for chapel. Next."

Robert had only attended a few church services while at Erdington and a few more with his primary school but he did not even know what the word denomination meant, let alone which one he belonged to if any. The following Sunday, he was shipped off to the local Methodist hall. The Methodists did not meet in the big church with the long drive, stained glass windows and paintings of Jesus. To get to the Methodist chapel, you had to walk down a long corridor next to a shop. There was a smoking room where old men smoked pipes and women drank tea. The smell of tobacco smoke stayed with Robert longer than any of the hymns or sermons.

These early memories of attending church did not diminish as Robert continued his nightly vigils reading and copying the Bible. He had been working unremittingly for some months, and now felt moved to go to church. But which one? He still didn't feel able to go into the beautiful Anglican church, so he opted for the small Gospel Hall in Jiggins Lane, just a short walk from Stonehouse Lane.

"It was little more than a hut with a corrugated roof," explains Robert. "The membership consisted of a dozen people, although as many as fifty to sixty children went to Sunday School. One of the leaders, Mr Barnwell, greeted me warmly. I told him I had no specific church background, although as I was able to tell him a lot about the Bible, he looked confused. You see, I had memorised whole chapters and verses while copying it out."

At the end of the service, Mr Barnwell took the new boy aside. He was shocked at how dishevelled he looked. His clothes were dirty and stained. His hair was too long and his face unwashed. The boy said he was fifteen but still had some difficulty speaking clearly. Mr Bramwell asked: "Are you born again, Robert? Have you accepted Jesus as your Saviour?"

The phrase from the third chapter of John's Gospel when Jesus spoke about the need to be born again was familiar to Robert, but he was unsure whether or not he was born again, so he replied he was probably not. Mr Barnwell invited him to say a prayer, admitting he was a sinner and asking Jesus into his life, which Robert gladly repeated. When he finished, other members of the congregation came over to congratulate him, but Robert was confused. He felt he should have been aware of something special happening, but he could not help think his confession was said more to please Mr.

Barnwell, than a heartfelt acceptance of Jesus. He left Jiggins Lane feeling accepted, but puzzled.

A few weeks later, Robert was lying wide awake in his bed. It was after midnight. His father was still out. His siblings were scattered in different care homes. He thought about Mr Barnwell's question whether or not he was born again.

"I found myself starting to cry. Mr Barnwell's words came back to me. I had never considered myself a sinner, rather someone who had been sinned against. The darkness of the room increased my sense of loneliness and feeling of being unloved. I so desperately wanted to be loved. I slid out of bed onto my knees to pray. I don't know how long I knelt there, but my legs were numb. I raised my head and called upon Jesus to come into my life, to forgive me for what I had done wrong, and I accepted him as my Saviour. There on the cold, dirty floor of No. 335 Stonehouse Lane, the place which for so long as a child had been a living hell, I became a child of heaven.

"After the operation on my tongue, I had felt free. When I started to work at George Mason's I felt free. When I fought back against my father, I felt free. Now, I had accepted Jesus as my Saviour, I did not hear bells ring or see fireworks go off. I was still uncertain what it all meant. But I also felt truly free in a way that I had never felt freedom before."

"From the moment I knelt on the floor of my cold room and accepted Jesus as my Saviour, I became aware of a dimension of God and an ever-available Jesus I did not know before. From that moment, too, the Bible became a miracle book in my own soul. God had touched me supernaturally and my life would never be the same again."

A new life and death

I f the church finally found a home in Robert, it would not be long before he found a home in the church—literally. By now, his father was using No. 335 like a guest house, coming home late at night, leaving in the morning and only staying around long enough to collect rent money on the day his son was paid. Once he had seized Robert's salary, he left on the bus for Birmingham and perhaps then to Betty's residence in Wales, or a new girlfriend in the city. Robert had no idea. William Hicks made it clear he wanted his son's money, not his company. Their conversations were always brief. This miserable existence was broken by Robert's siblings making very welcome occasional visits home from Erdington, or from relatives who had agreed to take them in.

"My heart broke when I saw Jean for the first time after we were split up; she was a shadow of the bright young girl who had roamed the fields with me or giggled happily on our cinema visits," says Robert. "Jean struggled to overcome father's abuse and, later in life, would have difficulty forming lasting relationships with men. Yet, she turned out to be a wonderful mother who raised her own children singlehandedly. To me, Jean's life is a celebration of how a woman can raise six wonderful children of her own, against all the odds. I say again and again, Jean is my hero. Bernard also visited. He was the quiet one in our family. He wheezed a lot due to his asthma and his squint gave him problems until it was fixed when he was twenty-one. Like my speech, it was a problem a good parent would have had corrected in childhood."

Stonehouse Lane held too many painful memories, so when Robert was asked by the elders of Jiggins Lane to come in early on

Sunday mornings to light the small wood burner stove in the church, it gave him an idea. With his own set of keys, he could come and go as he pleased. It would be simple just to live in the church. All his belongings fitted into one paper bag and, if he was careful, he could become a secret tenant.

"The church had slowly become my family," explains Robert. "Shortly after I joined, I ended up in hospital but father never visited me once. I had been in bed all day with terrible pains in my side. Bernard was at home and when he saw how distressed I'd become, he ran to the public phone box to call an ambulance. It turned out I had appendicitis which had actually burst. I was sent to Blackwell Convalescent Home for three weeks. I had no clothes to wear except the hospital gown they supplied, so I wasn't allowed out in the garden. I had to remain in the ward where I was terribly bored.

"I begged Bernard to bring me clothes and he arrived the next day with some filthy rags he had found in a cupboard. When a young couple from the church visited, I was very embarrassed. We walked around the garden, me in my smelly rags. That memory—of needless poverty and deprivation which is the work of the devil not God—stuck with me for many, many years. In fact, it has never left."

After being baptised, Robert felt even more at home with the church and so enacted his plan to live secretly in the old tin hut in Jiggins Lane. After a few weeks, he was discovered. Rather than being asked to leave the fellowship as he feared, he was told by Mr Palmer, one of the elders, he could move in with him and his wife. This arrangement not

"There was a nice song at the children's club at the little tin hut church. It went, 'What can I give him, poor as I am? If I were a shepherd, I would bring a lamb. If I were a wise man, I would do my part. Yet what can I give him? Give him my heart!'"

only meant having a clean bed, clothes and regular meals—at half the rent his father charged—but it allowed Robert to experience real Christian love and kindness. Now his speech was improving dramatically, he felt more "normal" than at any time in his life.

His personal faith was steadily growing, aided by regular visits to a shop called Treasure Trove in Cotteridge. It sold second-hand books within the price range of an errand boy. Robert bought Bible commentaries and study books, as well as a dictionary and encyclopaedias. The operation on his tongue had unleashed a dam, sweeping knowledge into his brain through books and pamphlets he collected at every opportunity. He snapped up illustrated Victorian books, fascinated by their pictures and engravings. In fact, he still has many of these today and they have turned out to be a shrewd investment worth a considerable sum of money.

From an early age, Robert recognised the value of both the written word and images in helping the mind, as well as the soul, to grow. He had fallen in love with words as he copied the King James Bible, while the painting of Jesus he saw as a child had fired his imagination. Both were helping to nurture his faith in a God he first encountered in the sweeping fields around Bartley Green.

Unlike most people, Robert had been gifted with a well-balanced brain. His left-side is organised and calculating, which is why he excelled at mathematics and logic; his right-side is artistic and intuitive, a factor which fired his career in the retail and publishing industries. This unique combination has helped Robert to operate equally in two worlds while most people focus on one. It was a gift he would put to good use for the Lord many years later when he published a complete series of Bibles with Ladybird where pictures helped children learn the Word of God.

During this time, Robert started visiting other churches as well as the one in Jiggins Lane. One was called Northfield and the other,

Quarry Lane. Sometimes he went to attend the Bible study or to hear a visiting speaker. He used his grocer's boy bike to get from one meeting to another, whizzing along country lanes and streets. One time he went flying over the handlebars at a sharp junction, almost killing himself. Bible studies, or what might now be better known in many churches today as "home groups" were opportunities to study, debate and learn Scripture in a way that was not possible on a Sunday morning.

"When I became a Christian, like many people, I grew slowly in the Lord," adds Robert. "Although I knew I was saved, I did not change overnight. We are called to be disciples which means continuing to grow in faith until the day we go to meet God face to face. We fall down now and then, but the Lord is always ready to forgive. I've not yet arrived, but I have left. I'm not yet where I want to be, but I'm not where I used to be either. When you accept Jesus, you enter into the most perfect relationship with the God of second, third and 200th chances. That relationship gives life meaning; but we are not yet perfect creatures.

"From the moment I knelt on the floor of my cold room and accepted Jesus as my Saviour, I became aware of a dimension of God and an ever-available Jesus I did not know before. From that moment, too, the Bible became a miracle book in my own soul. God had touched me supernaturally and my life would never be the same again."

Robert's morals, a word which did not reside naturally at No. 335, were also challenged. He always had a strong sense of right and wrong, all the more remarkable given the poor example he was set by his parents. Now his conscience would be tested when one of the elders, Mr Wise, announced he was going on holiday.

"Before he and his wife left, they gave me ten shillings—50p in today's money, and an enormous amount back then. They told me to buy some clothes as I always wore the same trousers and jumper. Instead, I treated myself to two visits to the cinema, some chocolate and fish and chips. I soon felt guilty, partly through my conscience troubling me and partly from the Bible warning against dishonouring elders.

"I used the last of the money to buy some clothes. As a result of the faith Mr and Mrs Wise put in me, I vowed to share whatever God gave me in my life. I believe God has given me a gift to make money and to use it responsibly and generously. I have not always lived up to that vow, but neither have I ignored it. Over the years, I have given a lot of money to individuals and ministries, a habit started with Mr and Mrs Wise planting the seed of ten shillings in me. Many years later, I would dedicate the 10 million Millennium Gospels to the memory of Mr Wise, one of the best Christian men I have ever met."

During these months, Robert's meetings with his father became less frequent. If he had to go home for any reason, the youngster would wait outside No. 335 until his father was asleep. The last place he expected an encounter with the man he often regarded as evil incarnate was in church.

One Sunday morning, William Hicks walked into Jiggins Lane, immediately befriending the elders and congregation. He spoke humbly, as one who missed his children, especially his son, Robert. Surely the church could understand the need for father and son to reconcile, he suggested. It was time to come home, he said to Robert. The elders were swayed by the tearful performance and advised Robert to move back with his distraught parent.

"It was a masterful performance from a very cunning man," he explains. "He even made out he was interested in learning about spiritual matters, but I knew all he wanted was my wages. I would gladly have given them to keep him from me. The church persuaded me to get back with my father and what a mistake it turned out to be.

I learnt that he had part-exchanged the house in Stonehouse Lane for a flat in Birmingham city centre.

"Gone were the green swathes of grass verges, the rolling hills and wide open space. These were replaced by concrete, traffic fumes and that acrid stench of the slums. I knew this could not be God's will. My father was trying to drag me back into an evil, sordid world from which I had escaped, just so he could have my wages and turn me into his unpaid servant. I spoke to my father about the Bible and Jesus on two occasions. I suppose he was the first person that I preached to. He did not want to talk about it at length, but I wanted him to know about how Jesus could turn anyone's life around."

Robert returned to Jiggins Lane church where the elders accepted his position. Mrs Andrews, the wife of the church's founder who had since died, offered him lodgings. He praised God for further evidence of his remarkable care.

A gifted retailer

Exceptional things were also happening in Robert's work life. He had started at George Mason's as a grocer boy. It was the lowest position in the shop, usually a job given to a schoolboy. His speech impediment, as well as his awkward shyness and pauper-stained clothes, should have held him back. Yet his superiors quickly noticed his industriousness, loyalty and easy charm with customers. He had always preferred the company of adults to other children and, after years of watching from the silent wings of life, had developed an astuteness for assessing people's characters and desires. In short, Robert had a natural talent for that old retail maxim—"Give the customer what the customer wants."

Supermarkets today are well-oiled, multinational institutions and a part of every High Street. People take self-service checkouts and two-for-one offers, not to mention impulse buys and end-of-line sales, for granted. But back in 1956, doing the routine grocery shop was a very different matter. Firstly a lack of fridges and freezers in most households meant people, usually housewives, shopped every day. There were no wide aisles, chip-and-pin or loyalty cards. Customers at George Mason's handed over their shopping lists to staff, took a seat at the counter, and then waited while their items were brought to them. There was also the option of the grocer boy making a home delivery.

As he climbed the retail ladder, Robert Hicks—the boy dismissed as retarded—would introduce many of the well-known and widely accepted shopping habits that are now part of everyday retail life. He pioneered what were then unique and radical innovations and his training ground was George Mason's Family grocers. His breakthrough came when the provisions manager left to work on the buses, leaving the post open to Robert. It was the chance he needed.

"That was the moment I can pinpoint as to when I really started to rise up in the world of retailing," he explains. "I was determined to be better than the man I replaced, better than anyone in the business. I had been studying how things had been done and had loads of my own ideas to improve business. One change I introduced involved pre-cutting food like bacon and cheese. Customers normally had to instruct staff how much they wanted, and then wait for the piece to be weighed and priced. It sounds simple, but my method ensured that when people came in, there was always a pre-cut piece available, saving customers waiting in a queue. It also freed up staff for other duties.

"Another change involved a housewives' favourite, ham on the bone. I would have it available on the counter, pre-sliced and without the usual amount of unwanted fat. Customers loved the idea and profits soared. I was still officially an apprentice, so head-office was shocked to learn the new ideas were mine. It wasn't normal to send an apprentice to work as a relief provisions manager in other shops but they were so delighted with my efforts, I was dispatched. I introduced the same ideas wherever I went, pushing up profits in the process.

"I was sent to George Mason's own training school where they taught you things such as where different types of tea came from and what ingredients were best suited to different cakes. Soon I was winning in-store competitions for selling the most products for a particular range and even for my window dressing. By the time I was eighteen, I was promoted to the role of Master Grocer and starting to shine among my peers.

"My speech was now as clear as anyone else's, so this provided me with extra confidence. I had come into my own, using and developing God-given talents and being supported by my bosses. I felt more fulfilled."

Robert's skills were also being recognised within the church. He had such an in-depth knowledge of Scripture, he soon earned a reputation as a biblical scholar. This amused him since he had left school at fifteen without a single qualification—and barely able to talk. Such was his reputation that pastors and congregations referred to him as simply the Boy Preacher. He was as keen to speak at Sunday Schools as he was to preach in a traditional tent crusade.

Robert was finding God's will for his own life, a life which had started in such bleak poverty, neglect and violence. He believed that being made in God's image meant God's will is for every individual to become more like him in every part of their lives. He knew his spiritual life was not supposed to be relegated to a God slot that's separate from all other parts of life.

"The will of God is for us to become like him and to know him more intimately in every area of our life. We don't need a special revelation to tell us that, and the details of how we do it are secondary. The specific will of God is contained within the talents he has given us. If God has given you the talent to be a plumber, why try and be a school teacher?

"I had a gift for preaching. Looking back, I suppose I spoke too fast and tried to cram too much into a sermon. Today, I speak more slowly and focus on one text the Lord has shown me, unless I am doing expository teaching or teaching students in Bible college. Preaching should not be about entertainment. I knew God was operating in my life, guiding and instructing me. How I behaved at work was just as important as how I behaved in church. I could not have two separate lives. I needed to act with integrity behind the shop counter as much as when I stood in the pulpit. That way I could love him more and show his love to everyone I met.

"The best way to learn God's will for us is to read the Word. I began to realise the Bible was the most important thing in my life, in anyone's life. The tin chapel at Jiggins Lane would one day rust and fall down. The other churches made of stone and stained glass would also crumble eventually. Even the love and fellowship of the congregation would end as they died or moved away. Only the Bible, and the truths it contains, was permanent. In the Gospel of Matthew (chapter 24, verse 35), Jesus said: 'Heaven and earth shall pass away, but my words shall not pass away.' That is the key."

On the brink of eternity

In a quiet, still room, William Hicks' life was passing away. He was only in his early fifties, but his body was riddled with cancer. Robert was shocked by his father's skeletal frame and the loud, gasping breaths and endless coughs which chimed regularly as if he had the very death knell swinging in his chest.

For years, William had had little contact with his children. He turned up once at Robert's door to borrow money. When he returned a week later for more, his son told him he would first have to pay back what he owed. William left.

Two weeks before their father died, Robert and Jean stood beside his bed, Robert just hidden in the shadows. Gloom dominated the room.

Sensing he was dying, the father turned to his daughter, feebly stretching out his hand, half in hope, half in a plea.

"Jean, I love you," he moaned.

As his daughter bent low to hear her father's words, his fingers accidentally brushed against her breast.

"No, not like that, not like that," the father sighed contritely.

The daughter stood quietly as her father tried to whisper something. But his voice was too weak or the words lived in a memory from too long gone.

"I knew I was witnessing a confession of sorts, a confession of a great evil which lingered still in my father's conscience," says Robert. "That greater sin blinded him to the needs of his sons who had also been sinned against, yet no plea for forgiveness came their way and they saw no signs of remorse for how he had treated them. Whether my father died at peace with God or not, I do not know. If he did, then he is in heaven. That is what the Bible teaches. I am not his judge. I do not condemn him. I do not hold a grudge. I am not bitter. I leave my father to the mercy of God."

As William's condition worsened, Robert was too numb to feel any real emotions. Brian took to looking after their father, washing and feeding him like a baby. One day, Brian was shaving his father when he suddenly stopped; lifting his arm, he slapped his father's face once, then twice. With tears in his eyes, he said: "Now you know what it's like to be hit when you are totally helpless."

The son then fetched clean pyjamas and a bucket. He cleaned his father's soiled body and changed the sheets. It was a task he performed until the day his father died.

Robert paid for the funeral.

Robert and Joyce on their wedding day.

Joyce

Jumping out of the old Bedford van, Robert almost tumbled into the arms of the prettiest girl he had ever seen. She was slim with soft blue eyes and a bright smile. She was wearing a bright yellow dress and was just eighteen. Three days later, Robert proposed, she accepted and they would be married for twenty-eight years

Her name was Joyce Robinson and, like Robert, she was spending a week at a Christian hotel in Scotland. He had travelled up from Birmingham with some friends in an old van, while Joyce had come with members of her church in Manchester. The Isle of Cumbrae off Scotland's west coast was beautiful in the July sunshine but Robert, now twenty, preferred the vision standing before him at the check-in desk. This girl captivated him, not just because of her looks but also her intelligence and her obvious love for Jesus.

The following day the pair joined other young people on a walk around the island's main town, Millport. They managed to fall behind, engrossed in each other's company and talking about everything and anything. Joyce said she attended a Grammar school in Manchester and was waiting for her A-Level results which she passed with distinction. She was extremely smart, warm and confident. Robert felt uncouth in her presence, yet they fitted comfortably together and soon the pair became a couple.

"Joyce wore makeup which was almost considered heresy in her church so I teased her terribly," he says. "On the second day we were together, something inside me told me this was the woman I was going to marry. I was immensely attracted to her and we shared a deep faith. I loved hearing Joyce talk about her faith and her church; her love of Jesus shone in her manner and her speech. I proposed on our third day together and when she accepted, I was overjoyed.

"Joyce was the first person who loved me. Other people had been kind, some very kind to me. The love of a strong fellowship such as I had experienced in church was extremely satisfying. But the love Joyce felt for me and I for her was different. I thought I was unlovable, then this beautiful, intelligent and God-fearing woman told me she loved me. I couldn't believe it. Not me, with all my faults and issues, but she did."

Robert believed God's hand was on their relationship from the start. He had been invited on the holiday by Mr and Mrs Ainsley and, at the time, was still working at George Mason's earning extra money as a relief manager. A stint in another shop would pay for the holiday to Scotland as he split his regular salary between his rent, living expenses and a donation to renovation work at Quarry Lane Gospel Hall. Three weeks before he was due to leave for Scotland, there was no relief work in sight. The holiday appeared to be doomed. Robert prayed, and then he received a call at the last moment, asking him to fill in for a manager during the two weeks before his holiday. It was indeed a Godsend.

A few months later when he and Joyce were preparing to get married, he told her that he had saved £50 for their wedding and first house, a tidy sum even then. However, Robert had pledged £50 to the Quarry Lane church before he met his fiancée.

Robert adds: "Joyce said, 'If you've made a vow to God, Bobby, you must keep that vow. The money belongs to him, not us.'"

He was impressed by this strong faith. How many brides-to-be would put the welfare of their church ahead of their big day, he wondered. That week, Mason's announced a window-dressing competition among its four hundred stores, with a first prize of £50.

Robert set up a dazzling display—and came second, winning £25. Two close friends gave them £25 as a wedding present, followed by £50 from Joyce's parents. Robert realised this was God's blessing as he had received his £50 back with 100% interest.

After they married, Mr and Mrs Hicks waited patiently on a promise from Mason's to give them a flat above Robert's own shop. By the winter of 1962, Joyce was pregnant with their first child. Robert was managing a shop but it did not come with a flat so he rented an attic apartment nearby.

"That winter was very cold with heavy snow falling over a period of several days. One night, Joyce and I were in bed when suddenly the roof caved in. We were covered in thick freezing snow. Then a coin stuck in the gas meter. Fortunately we had a small electric fire. I still remember us huddling together, trying to stay warm while any heat from that little fire vanished through the gaping hole in the ceiling. It was like a scene from a West End farce, but my heavily pregnant wife could still smile and keep me laughing. We thanked the Lord that we at least had one another, if not any tiles on the roof.

"We used to hold weekly Bible studies in our flat with two other couples. It was a wonderful time, sharing God's Word with them. We learnt so much, not least the importance of good Christian friendship."

God's provision and care was remarkably evident at that time. Mason's were still delaying over a flat and Robert was anxious to give his new wife a roof—quite literally—over her head and continue his climb up the retail ladder. He prayed for a sign, asking God to give him a decision on their accommodation by noon the following Monday. At the same time, the landlord of the attic flat gave the couple notice to vacate it by the end of the month.

"Ten minutes before noon, I still hadn't heard anything, so I phoned Mason's personnel department. The manager was very surprised to hear my voice. He said he was just about to phone to inform me a shop had finally come up, with a flat attached. It was in Selly Oak near Birmingham. The moving-in date was the very week we were due to leave our attic flat. Once again, God had met our needs."

Busy at work

The next few years were an exciting and profitable time for the ambitious young manager. With his own shop to run, Robert's natural flair for sales and meeting customer needs saw turnover soar from £300 a week to £450. But then came disaster. Head office announced they were closing the Selly Oak branch and transferring business to Bourneville, three miles away. There was a lot of competition from other grocers, not least the Co-Op, and Mason's wanted to consolidate business in the larger outlet.

This news made Robert determined to increase his shop's turnover even more, to save it from closure. He introduced a number of sales initiatives including his new ideas for special offers, two-for-one purchases and promotions which were unheard of in the early 1960s. Robert was forty years ahead of his time. Shopping in Britain had remained virtually unchanged in decades. This enterprising manager turned the industry on its head and came up smiling and with profitability

"I dreamed today that I was a good boy and that everybody wanted to talk and to listen to me. I dreamed I was living in a big house with a big kitchen with lots of hot food. I know it was only a dream but I liked it very much. Maybe one day, the dream will come true. But I'm not sure."

every time. Soon turnover doubled to £600 a week and he set himself a target of £1,000, an unheard of target for such a small shop.

"I would badger the big brand-makers like Andrex, who produced toilet rolls, to introduce a cheaper one. They were reluctant at first but I persuaded them to see how it would help increase their profits. Soon everyone was doing it. Sugar was a popular purchase, so I put special offers with all sugar purchases. I put a cheaper product with a quality product on special offer and kept pushing up the volume. People couldn't get enough.

"The most revolutionary thing I did was to change the store layout. A new chain store was opening up across Britain. It was called Tesco. It was probably the first retailer to make the jump from shops to supermarkets, letting people wander round the premises, choosing items themselves and bringing them to new tills called checkouts where they could pay. I ripped out the old counter in George Mason's where the customers sat on their stools. I stacked our products next to special offers and put hand-made price tags on them. The customers loved it. One day, Mr Weston, Mason's inspector, came in, saw the counter was missing and customers helping themselves rather than waiting patiently on their seats. He exclaimed: 'You can't do that!' and I replied, 'I just have.' He changed his mind when he saw the figures for that week's turnover were nudging £900. I had tripled the shop's income."

Mr Simmonds, one of George Mason's directors, made a personal visit to the Selly Oak store which had become the talk of the boardroom; in fact, Robert's nickname was "The Golden Boy". He reversed the closure decision, telling Robert his shop would be transformed into a new self-service facility. The shop was now breaking the £1,000 a week target, earning its manager the biggest bonus Mason's had ever paid, even more than the inspectors received. Robert was asked to oversee a new shop in another town but he was unhappy with the small pay rise he was offered. He felt his talents were not being properly rewarded. Besides, he already had one eye on Tesco which his astute business sense recognised as being at the forefront of the shopping revolution. When a manager's vacancy in Coventry arose, he applied for it and was taken on. His career had taken another twist, one that would provide both rewards and problems.

The atmosphere at George Mason's had always been that of a family business. Robert had a lot of freedom to operate his store as he saw fit. At Tesco he found business was more centrally controlled. When he occasionally messed up at Mason's, a named manager from head office would call and ask, "Bobby, what went wrong?' With his new boss, it was very different. After Robert (without telling his superiors) promoted one deal involving a coupon in the local paper, he received a curt telephone call. An unknown voice from Tesco headquarters asked: "Mr Hicks, have you costed the price of this promotion? Please do not do this again. We are in charge of press advertising."

Robert remained undeterred. He knew his customers. He knew, for example, most local people could not afford butter, relying instead on soft margarine. It was also popular with housewives making sandwiches for their husbands' work. Robert agreed a deal with a manufacturer to buy margarine in bulk, receiving a discount for every ten boxes purchased. Two weeks later, Tesco's chief buyer telephoned, extremely annoyed at the large invoice she had just received from the margarine supplier. "Mr Hicks, we have never sanctioned such a huge quantity in any of our shops. You should not have made such a large order. I have instructed the supplier to send a lorry to your shop to collect the margarine."

Robert just smiled: "You can send the lorry, but there may be a problem."

"What problem?" asked the buyer.

"Well, I've sold all the margarine. There's none left."

The buyer did not believe what the young manager told her, so she sent an inspector round to double check. It was true. Robert's ability to supply on the demand of his customers had proved itself once again. His mathematical mind could hold dozens of different prices at any one time, bamboozling even the most experienced buyer. Tesco paid even closer attention to what he did, not to reprimand, but to copy his marketing prowess in more of their stores. He was in his element and he was not yet twenty-five years old.

Robert knew it was important to study the international food markets up close. With the Russian-American cold war at its height, supplies of Alaskan red salmon dried up. It was a popular Sunday treat for families in Birmingham, a step up from cheaper tuna. Whenever a relative came round for Sunday lunch, children were sent to the grocers to buy red salmon. Cold war tensions meant the trade magazines were predicting the price of salmon would go sky high, placing the item beyond the reach of most shoppers. Robert waited until the price was about to rocket, then bought hundreds of cases. He sat on those for six weeks until the price eventually went through the roof. Now Robert could start selling the salmon at more than the previous price but still at an affordable rate. Tesco bosses were astounded.

He took risks and, almost always, they paid off. He was afraid of no one and loved the excitement of his business. He was not just dealing with tins of salmon; he was working with housewives' habits, people's lifestyles, the economy, and even international politics. It made for an interesting day at the office.

The secret of success

In the midst of his material and business success, Robert was careful not to allow it to blind him to the real meaning of that word. Sure, he loved bartering with suppliers and thinking up new customer initiatives. He got a thrill seeing a housewife select his latest offer and sending increased turnover figures to head office. He thrived on this success, but he was careful that it did not rule his life, or interfere with his love of God.

"Over the years I have enjoyed a good share of success. I have also endured a number of failures. Only a few people make a real difference to the world and then only for a short while. Someone like Bill Gates changed the way most of us work, thanks to Microsoft. But there will come a time when his achievements will be considered mundane and overtaken by more advanced technological developments.

"Only one person has had what I would call ultimate success and that person is Jesus. He changed the world. More than 2,000 years after he walked on the earth, he is still changing the world and people's hearts. There has been no one like him. He is a one-off. He's THE Managing Director, CEO and Head of Department rolled into one. Any other success in the world's eyes pales into insignificance with what Jesus has done. I know.

"Success in life is not down to whether I make a lot of money or have to scrape by. I will be judged by him on whether I did the father's will. Did my material success make me a more loving person, or a greedier, selfish person? The world equates success as having lots of money, a nice house, an expensive car and overseas holidays. That is so shallow. If material success leads to addiction, unhappiness and broken relationships as it has done for many celebrities, then it isn't worthy of the name success. That is failure; failure to be human, to love one's neighbour and, above all, to love God."

Shopping

While the image of the Swinging Sixties is often one of a country enjoying one long party, the reality in big industrial cities such as Birmingham was very different. Poverty still trapped many people. The post-war recovery had not filtered through to everyone. Many families struggled to pay their rent or buy life's basics such as food and clothing. Working for a supermarket brought Robert into contact with all sorts of people. Some of those he remembers most were the shoplifters. There were scammers, of course, who stole valuable items to order and then sold them on the black-market or down at the local pub. There were others who regarded shoplifting as a way of life. One pregnant lady became a regular customer and was very friendly with staff until someone pointed out she had been expecting her baby for rather a long time—more than nine months. When she was taken aside and her jacket opened, it was discovered her "baby bump" was actually half a laundry basket strapped to her waist which she filled from the shelves on every trip.

The tragic cases were those which saddened Robert. These were the shoplifters simply trying to feed their families. One of the saddest incidents he can recall involved a mother of two who was caught red-handed. At the time, he was an inspector for Tesco in charge of twenty shops. Called to the manager's office in one large store, he saw a terrified woman sitting between two burly security guards. The official procedure was to involve the police, but this woman's face haunted Robert.

"She had bruises on her cheeks and below her eyes. She begged me not to call the police or her husband would knock her about. I could see he had already done so. It brought back terrible memories. I asked the security guards to leave us alone but they refused. Those guys were a law unto themselves. I persisted and told them they could report me to head office if they liked.

"When we were alone, I assured the woman who was now in tears that I would not report her. Instead, I phoned a church near where she lived, insisting she accepted whatever help they offered. She said she would but I did not check up on her. I believe every case ought to be taken on its own merits. I don't think people at the bottom of the pile should be trampled on. They need a chance. We serve a merciful God who gives us chance after chance. He gives us what we need, not what we deserve."

A few hours later, Robert received his reprimand from head office, but he did not mind.

*****

At home, Robert and Joyce's family were increasing. By the time he left Tesco for a huge new challenge at the Co-Op, the couple had four children: Andrew, Peter, Julia and Joanna. Another child miscarried, although it was three months before Joyce realised. She was taken to hospital, the dead child's body removed and Joyce given a massive blood transfusion.

Home life was chaotic but fun. There literally was never a dull moment. The children were encouraged to bring friends round, often children who went to their church or Sunday School. Yet, Robert and Joyce had a heart to foster more children, with a dozen or more passing through their doors over the years.

The cheeky boy and the sparkling girl in the yellow dress he met when he was falling out of an old van were still very much in love and, every day, growing in the Lord.

Robert at his desk.

Business man

Robert was excited about his new job. It was a tremendous, groundbreaking challenge. The only problem was he did not have a clue where to start.

The Co-Op had shocked the media by announcing it was to open a new superstore called a hypermarket on the Wirral, in Merseyside. It would not only sell food, but also clothes, furniture, jewellery, household goods and electrical appliances. The company had been losing ground to the meteoric rise of Tesco and believed a hypermarket was the way forward. The huge Wirral complex would break the mould for shopping and be the biggest revolution the retail industry had ever known. Robert saw an advert for the position of Director of this new enterprise—which also involved looking after one hundred and ten shops—and applied. He had been unhappy for some time in his job with Tesco. This was an opportunity to move on to a new challenge, something he always relished.

The Co-Op had bought a disused laundry, measuring a massive 80,000 square feet. The director, Mr Murdoch, had a vision for a new way of shopping but needed someone to make that vision a reality. Robert was called for an interview which meant travelling north to Liverpool. His heart sank as he drove through a rundown area. Memories of the Birmingham slums of his childhood flashed before his mind; the deprivation and neglect, which went unreported behind so many cracked doors and boarded up windows, saddened his heart. It was when he reflected how God had blessed him, taken him out of that misery, led him to an amazing woman, given them four wonderful children and how he was now heading for an interview for the prime retailing job in the country (even though he still could not spell), that Robert stopped the car and there, by the side of the road, thanked the Lord.

"I was asked to return for a second interview, this time with Mr Murdoch alone. I spoke about marketing and of the need to start where the customer was and not where the Co-Op was. The talk in the industry was the post would go to an internal candidate, so there were more than a few gasps in retail boardrooms across the country, when Mr Murdoch awarded it to me, the man from Tesco.

"On the drive home, I realised there was one huge problem: I had no idea where to start. The hypermarket was a completely new venture. There was no model to follow. As well as managing the hypermarket, I had overall responsibility for managing one hundred and ten Co-Op shops. It was the mother of all challenges. I was ready for it."

As he undertook this new role, Robert wanted to ensure his other roles—as a father and preacher—would not suffer. He may be working for mammon but he served God first. He saw a parallel between the position of manager at the hypermarket and his position as a father. He did not have a proper role model for either venture. It would be too simple to look at how his own father had behaved and then do the opposite. With the children growing up fast, Robert faced many dilemmas: how much should he discipline them and in what way? How much time should he spend with them? He seemed to have more questions than answers; thankfully, the Lord had also blessed him with the world's most understanding and patient wife and mother.

"My instinct told me to put the children first. I wanted them to have every opportunity but I did not want to spoil them. I'm someone who gives one hundred per cent to anything or anyone, and it was that way with my children. One aspect of my own childhood which I did bring to them was my love for stories. I made sure the stories I told had sound morals. Joyce introduced family Bible reading and prayer, and we took them to church.

"Neither Joyce nor I had any precedent of Christian family life to work with. We were both first-generation Christians, although Joyce did come from a very loving family. My biggest fear was that I would hit our children like my father had done to me and my siblings. To counter this, I spent long hours in prayer and Bible reading. I found these activities strengthened my ability to be a good parent. My earthly father may not have been a good example, but my Heavenly Father has never let me down."

When Joyce was seven months pregnant with her fourth child, Joanna, she was in the car with Robert driving. He got stuck at a junction and another vehicle smashed into their side, flipping them over. No one was seriously injured although Robert did have a seizure. The next day he attended a speaking engagement which he knew he should have cancelled but he was too stubborn. Robert was now a family man. He was no longer the Boy Preacher but a man with responsibilities. He knew God was still calling him to speak and give lectures, but he needed to cut back and turn down invitations which took him out of the house several days a week or overnight. God was directing him to family life and a business career, to developing skills and talents which he would soon use to direct millions of people to the God he had discovered when he was just a fifteen-year-old boy in a dirty kitchen, through a book that was then 350 years old: the King James Version of the Bible.

Fostering

The Hicks household was rarely without the sound of children laughing, playing, reading Scripture, praying and, occasionally, fighting over toy soldiers or dolls' prams. It was a happy, ordinary home where love, warmth and chocolate biscuits were always in plentiful supply. Joyce wanted to be a full-time mum while encouraging her husband in his many business ventures. She provided the solid family foundations; Robert worked long hours to keep the finances rolling in. At night, they shared their joys and woes in prayer while their extended family continued to grow.

The couple had once been approached by someone at church to consider fostering children over short periods. This often involved youngsters whose parents were in hospital or had been temporarily removed from their families through neglect or abuse. Robert had a big heart for those children while Joyce had a natural mothering instinct for all kinds of children. One youngster who left a lasting impression was two-year-old Mark.

Robert explains: "When he arrived, Mark did not interact with anyone, spending all his time alone in a corner of the room. He was still in nappies. He never laughed or smiled. It was our daughters, Julia and Joanna, who finally won him over after nearly two months. Slowly, little Mark came out of his shell, smiled for the first time and enjoyed being hugged. After a year, he was returned to his mother and, as one of the rules of fostering was for there to be absolutely no contact with the children when they left foster parents, we never discovered what happened to this shy little boy."

Another family who affected them greatly were three sisters. Two were toddlers, while the

"What is a friend? It must be someone who does not expect to gain anything from you, but wants to be with you whenever he can. Maybe no one in the world has a real friend. I don't think I will ever have a friend. I wonder if I could be a real friend to somebody. One day, I will try."

eldest was around six. Their father had remarried after his wife died but the stepmother did not want children so they were placed in care. Robert delighted all three children with his storytelling abilities, and would take them on excursions. After six months, a couple were identified as suitable parents and, following more paperwork, the Hicks were told the girls would be taken from them in two weeks.

Robert adds: "On the handover day, the three girls refused to come out of the house. They cried in a way I've never heard children cry before or since. They clung to Joyce and me. It broke our hearts to put them in the other couple's car and see them leave. We knew this couple were good parents, but that didn't make the goodbyes any easier. We had tried to adopt them ourselves but were pipped to the post.

"We always prayed for the children we fostered. Prayer has a real power non-believers don't understand. It brings protection and dynamism into the lives of another human being. Fostering gave Joyce and me the opportunity to love unconditionally. We did not choose the children who came to us but we loved them all equally. Jesus said it is easy to love those who love us. The challenge is to love everyone, even those we find it hard to love.

"It's our job to love people as they are—which is how God loves us. When you look through a camera lens, you see things differently. Love is the lens through which you love people. You'll see attractiveness in everyone the moment you start looking; but if you wait for it to appear, you'll be disappointed."

A new retail venture

The hypermarket in the Wirral was being prepared for its grand opening. The race was on to beat a similar project by a rival supermarket in Wales. The media loved this brave new world of super shopping but Robert felt the Co-Op lacked the necessary public relations and marketing skills to keep one step ahead of the competition. While the giant shell was fitted out, Robert was also operating as marketing manager of the Birkenhead and District Co-Op with overall responsibility for well over one hundred and ten shops. He told Mr Murdoch the chain needed to introduce three main changes.

These were to alter the pricing structure of its produce; secondly, to improve the packaging of its own brand products to make them more attractive; and thirdly, to introduce family-sized packs alongside the smaller, more expensive tins intended for pensioners. There was one other change needed: the advertising undertaken by the Co-Ops was standard, boring and information-oriented, rather than sales-led. This last change brought Robert into direct conflict with the advertising agency which held the Co-Op account. He became a lone voice against outdated retail marketing which he believed kept the chain well behind its competitors. For example, he felt the advertising budget was largely wasted as it was spent on buying space in newspapers which were mainly read by men. However, research showed it was wives who decided how to spend the housekeeping money. That's when Robert launched the country's first free weekly paper full of shopping coupons. It was another master stroke. At first, there was some resistance, but his ideas were eventually taken on board and turnover rose sharply. Once again, his innate understanding of the retail business was proved to be exactly right.

Robert worked on every aspect of the new hypermarket. He knew that many customers used to small corner shops would feel lost in a giant building with a maze of aisles and shelving, so he designed a shop within a shop, another feature commonly used today. That meant separate counters for the butchers, bakery and fishmonger. He visited France where hypermarkets were a common feature but did not feel the narrow aisles and shelves stocked to the ceiling would work in Britain. Instead, he ordered the Wirral aisles be made wider. Robert was giving birth to a whole new concept for retail sales, and the competition was watching intently.

"We opened Britain's first hypermarket a few weeks ahead of the one in Wales," he says proudly. "It was a frantic time to get things ready. We were working round the clock right up to the last minute. The overall verdict of the media, the trade and, most importantly, the customer, was one of success. Not everything worked and, in the succeeding weeks, we continued to make changes. But we did it. I was proud of my achievements, not least as I was the former grocer's boy labelled a failure even before he left school. If only those teachers could have seen me that day, standing in the middle of the giant hypermarket surrounded by television cameras, newspaper reporters and thousands of expectant customers. It was quite a sight. I was the man behind the biggest change in Britain's shopping culture in decades. It just proves what Scripture states: God really is no respecter of persons."

Keeping faith fresh

If Robert was leading a retail revolution, his religious revolution was not far behind. While working on the Wirral, he met up with a group of Christian businessmen who, with Robert, were organising a tent crusade. On the committee was Eric Bell, chairman and managing director of Blakes, a large car franchise group in Birkenhead, with Robert directing strategy and marketing. He and Robert became friends from their first meeting.

They knew the traditional tent revival itself needed reviving. Basically, the saving message of Jesus did not need to change; it was just the method of delivering it which had to be refreshed. It was no longer enough just to run a series of evening meetings and expect people to attend, not least due to the rise of television and the cinema. Robert and Eric decided to turn the tent into an exhibition of Christian missionary societies and invited schools to come and hear about their overseas work. They also put on a puppet show organised by the Liverpool City Mission. Robert had visited Capernwray Bible College in north Lancashire which had an excellent reputation for turning out first-class students and preachers. He invited the staff to send some of its students to address RE classes and assemblies in Liverpool's schools before and after the crusade. The students also got involved in practical evangelism, such as painting church halls and visiting the housebound. With her children at school, Joyce was able to play a role. She also helped organise intensive Bible Schools which ran over a six-week period.

Robert also had his sights on the churches where the Sunday services had been trundling on in the same manner for decades until they fossilised into religious practices, rather than Spirit-filled sessions. He got young people to act out dramas based on biblical stories such as the Prodigal Son in which the young man was transformed into a rich footballer who had allowed his skills to fall away through addictions to alcohol and fame. It was an easily understood parable on football-mad Merseyside and a fresh retelling of Jesus' parables without losing the integrity of their message.

The format for services also came under Robert's scrutiny. It is common today for churches to start their services with five or six praise songs, something not so familiar in the 1960s when the usual pattern of a service involved a "hymn-prayer-hymn sandwich" as the norm. Robert changed that, too. Even more radical was a question-and-answer session he encouraged churches to hold. Attendances in the churches where these ideas were encouraged rose sharply and many people came to the Lord in repentance and faith.

"It's no good having the world's greatest message if it's packaged in a way people cannot understand or identify with," explains Robert. "You can use different means to spread the gospel without losing or endangering the gospel's truth.

"I realised the customer is always right, even in a church situation. If people leave the service the same way as they come in, then something is wrong. I once heard a man say that before he became a Christian, he lived opposite a church. On Sunday morning, he watched the people walk in looking as though they were going to the dentist; when they left, they looked like they had been at the dentist. That's not how Jesus would have worked. Experimenting, and even failing, is not wrong. It's better to have tried than simply carry on as it's always been done.

"I learnt in retail that the best way to test a new product is to test-launch it in one area. That's how Christians should work. Rather than seeking God's will, maybe we should try out something in order to see if it is God's will. What works in one area may not work in another."

Launching out alone

Robert had never been busier and had never felt more fulfilled. He was seeing his childhood dream of telling people about the Bible come to fruition; his family and children were his delight; his business enterprises were flourishing. So it seemed unthinkable he would decide to leave his job with the Co-Op to start his own business, marketing a new labelling device he had invented. At the time, most supermarkets labelled their produce with stickers stuck flat on the shelves. Robert's concept, which he called Project-o-Price, used bright, colourful labels projecting from the shelves, making items more attractive and eye-catching. It was a simple yet highly effective method which would fundamentally change the way pricing was done in every supermarket in the country.

"I wanted to market Project-o-Price and what I should have done was work through the Co-Op. Instead, I told Mr Murdoch I was leaving to set up my own company to sell the system. He was flabbergasted, begging me to stay. I wouldn't listen—maybe it was pride or maybe it was just I didn't think things through. Maybe I should have prayed more, asking God for guidance rather than rushing forward with my own decision. Mr Murdoch sent his wife round to speak to Joyce in a bid to stop me leaving. Other people tried to talk me out of my plan, but I was determined."

Robert went into partnership with a manufacturer before the reality of his decision hit home. It would be a long time before he saw any return on his investment. With a wife and family of four to support, he needed to start earning a salary. He began working as a retail consultant with his first client, a supermarket in Iceland. A cash-and-carry operation in Manchester offered him a job, but he soon learnt that wholesale was a completely different enterprise from retail. Another job offer arose, this time in Hull. Robert's reputation in the retail industry was second to none and once it was known his services were available, he was head-hunted by other companies. However, Hull was on the other side of the country and he was reluctant to move his family again as they were settled on the Wirral. He continued to select the consultancy jobs which suited him best to earn enough money to support his family.

"Your mother phoned last night."

One business trip to America had been particularly tiring. He had spent ten days living out of a suitcase pursuing a number of contracts, none of which was finalised. To make matters worse, his plane circled Chicago for two hours because of air traffic control problems—which made him miss his London connection. Robert was looking forward to seeing Joyce and the children. He was overjoyed when he finally landed and Joyce was waiting with the car at Heathrow.

Tired and jetlagged, he settled into the passenger seat. As Joyce drove through the main exit tunnel of the airport, she turned to her husband.

"I'm glad you're sitting down, Robert. I have some news for you."

"What is it? Not problems with the children?"

"No. They're all well. It's something else."

"What, darling? What is it?"

"Your mother phoned last night."

Robert and Richard Bewes looking at the Ladybird Bible cover design.

A stranger returns

Two hours later, still jetlagged, Robert was travelling up the M1 to meet the mother who had walked out on her family twenty-eight years earlier. He still has no recollection how he managed to make that journey. Confusion, anger, indifference and disbelief were just some of the emotions he experienced at the time.

He thanked God that Joyce was driving them home from the airport as he was too shattered emotionally to do anything but sit in the car and brood over her words: "Your mother phoned last night."

When he arrived home, painful memories were still clamouring in his mind; it was as if his heart was being violently wracked with once-dormant recollections which had suddenly burst into life in an agonising new birth.

"Your mother phoned last night." The words still seemed unreal. He remembered the woman who collected him from the Erdrington Home when he was just six. That was mother. He remembered the woman who never spoke to her children unless it was to tell them to get out of her way. That was mother. He remembered the stone-faced woman leaving Bartley Green on the bus while little Jack wept uncontrollably at the window, begging her to stay. That was mother. She had left. Now she had returned.

"If I am honest, that day, I shared much with the second son in the parable of the Prodigal Son," admits Robert. "In some ways, we are all like him when it comes to forgiveness. While the father welcomed his long-lost son back with open arms, even though he had wasted all his inheritance, his brother's attitude was more like: 'So you're back. What do you want from me?'

"Unlike the rest of my family who had made some effort to trace her, I blotted out all memories of my mother. I had put the past behind me. I had made something of my life. I had a lovely family and been successful in business. I wanted to pray, but it was difficult. My mind was in turmoil."

When he arrived home, Joyce handed Robert a pad with the phone number in Northampton left by his mother. Northampton? It seemed so close for someone who had been so far away for so long. He dialled. She answered. All he can remember of their first conversation in three decades was one question he asked: "Are you alone?" For some reason, he expected his mother to be living with a man—perhaps the man for whom she had left her six children.

Winifred was now sixty-five. She had decided it was time to get back in touch with her family. She had managed to find Jean's telephone number. Jean was overjoyed to hear her mother's voice and insisted she stay with her. Robert was to drive to Northampton then take her to Jean's house in Birmingham. It was ironic that as the last person who wanted a reunion, Robert, was the first actually to meet his mother in the flesh.

"Hello, Bobby," she said as he walked into her house which she owned. Her packed suitcases stood beside her. Another terrible memory shuddered in his brain.

Robert did not know how or what to answer. He thought she looked smaller, ill and older than her age. She explained she had suffered from kidney problems and high blood pressure; her gall bladder had been removed. Robert could not bring himself to ask any personal questions such as, "Why did you abandon us, mother?" So he stuck with health and the weather.

A painful silence filled the car journey to Jean's. He was relieved as one by one his siblings arrived. Despite the short notice, eighteen of

Winifred's twenty-four grandchildren were on hand to kiss and greet her.

"Picking up the pieces after so many years wasn't easy," adds Robert. "There was a lot of forgiveness and healing required. The six of us handled it in our own way, but the acrimony, mostly apathy, towards the one who had abandoned us, slowly faded."

Over the next few days, Winifred told her story. When she left Bartley Green in 1952, she had just £4 in her pocket. That bought a bus ticket to London where she moved into a woman's hostel. As a young girl, she had attended a convent school in the capital but the faith she had been taught had long since been extinguished. After several years, a friend she worked with took her to church where some long-lost belief was given a few smouldering sparks.

Deciding she wanted to improve herself, Winifred enrolled in a property management class and was soon acting as an agent for a number of tenants. Later, Robert would also get involved with property management; he thought it ironic that the woman, whose very smell repulsed him, should shadow part of his career.

In 1965, his mother moved to Northampton where she ran a corner shop. Maybe it was something in the genes, but once again, both mother and son followed a similar business route. She remained there for ten years until the job became too much and she sold the business. It was then she began thinking about contacting her family but did not know where to begin.

> "I know inside my heart I cry a lot. No one can see the tears. I even cry inside when I am smiling on the outside. I don't want people to know I have been crying. When I grow up, I will never cry again, because when I am an adult, no one will be able to hurt me."

"I was so afraid of your father because I was sure he would kill me if he knew where I was," she told her assembled children. "That's why I didn't contact you. I thought all you children would be taken into care. I was sure you would be looked after by the council. I had no idea you would be allowed to stay with your father."

Robert told her how their dad had beaten the children nightly, trying to get information on where she was. They had suffered so she would not. She bowed her head.

"Bobby, I know you must hate me. All of you must. I was wrong to have abandoned you but I thought it was for the best. I was depressed. One day I snapped. I couldn't take our living conditions any more. I couldn't cope with the poverty and the abuse from your father. He made me do terrible things. I can't tell you. There was no reasoning with him. I fought my corner for years but he wore me down. That was when I knew I had to leave. I know I was never a good mother. I can't explain why. I was wrong. I missed you all but I thought it was for the best that someone else care for you. They could give you more than I ever could."

Winifred looked at her six children one by one. "I have lived a very colourful life. I have been selfish. Before I got in touch with all of you, I knew I needed to get back in touch with Jesus. I know he has forgiven me. I hope you do, too. I forgive those who harmed me, including your father. I am healed and I want to forget the past."

Roberts says: "That night, I gave my mother a Bible. Many times during our conversation, she said 'Thank God.' Neither I nor my siblings really knew if mother's confession was genuine. Her behaviour in the next few years seemed to throw doubt on her words. But, like my father, I am not her judge. I leave them to the mercy of God."

For the next few years, Winifred lived with different children on a rotating basis, including Robert, who also encouraged her to publish her own story. She died a few years later in a nursing home from a lung condition. She was seventy-one.

Following God's will in a new venture

Another chapter in his business life was about to close. Now he had left the Co-Op, Robert was becoming weary of his consulting work which was haphazard and took him away from home too much. He did not have the same excitement for wholesale. He accepted a managing director's post for a large wholesale company but had lost his desire for the whole industry. Rather than resign, he waited to be sacked which meant a generous severance package. It allowed him to pay off outstanding debts and have time to look—and pray—for a new challenge. But where?

The first step was prayer and consultation with the church elders. He felt God calling him to be more active in the church. He had been preaching and teaching in his spare time, sometimes meeting people who remembered him as the Boy Preacher. The church affirmed they would recommend Robert as a Bible teacher.

Then an elder phoned him about an advert he had seen for a marketing manager with Scripture Union. It was a temporary, six-month post involved with publishing and bookselling programmes. While Robert could sell salmon to Alaska, he admitted at his interview that he knew nothing about publishing. In addition, his dyslexia meant he could not spell. At the Co-Op, he had created an energetic staff and had his own PA thus enabling him to ensure the shops had hundreds of promotions operating at any one time. Robert must have convinced Scripture Union bosses that he was the man they were looking for. They offered him the job, an office and a secretary. Nigel Sylvester was then the General Secretary, eventually becoming the International Secretary for Scripture Union.

"This was a major commitment for me, because it meant taking a 70% pay cut and working during the week in London while Joyce cared for the children back in the Wirral," explains Robert. "I felt called to use my talents for the church and, above all, the Bible. I owed so much to Scripture. Now I wanted to get the Word into as many people's hands as I could and this job seemed the ideal way to achieve that."

Robert quickly learnt, however, that books are very different commodities from cornflakes. Once you've got the formula right for cornflakes, you've only got one product to sell. The real task is in marketing the cornflake, not reinventing it every month. With publishing, Robert was effectively dealing with new products on a regular basis, meaning he had to overcome numerous challenges.

"Even if you are an avid reader who always has to have a new book, you are going to choose from a very wide range of books that are as different as cornflakes are from roast beef. So, if a publisher has enough individual books that can make a profit, then he stays in business and is successful. But he has to approach the product and marketing in a different way. In fact, many authors only became really successful after their death. Once their books were out of copyright, a number of publishers would reproduce their works, and made them available at a relatively cheap price to a wider market."

Robert fell in love with Scripture Union from the first day. His old retail hunger had not disappeared—and that would often to be the source of friction with his new employers. He was humbled to have a team of dedicated staff who regarded their work as a vocation rather than simply a job. On the other hand, while they toiled as missionaries, he felt they lacked the retail professionalism he was used to. He wanted to commercialise the business of the SU but the SU was not in the business of commercialism. That was not how missionaries operated. It was to be a clash of ideas which would erupt time after time.

The clash of ideas

"Back then SU had its own chain of bookshops but I quickly detected that most managers did not have a strong sales mentality. For example, I introduced a three-weekly promotion which included windows and counter displays. It met with stiff resistance. My aim was to attract customers into the shops and show what a wide range of products was available. The managers expected people to come in just because it was a Christian bookshop. I saw a comparison with Tesco. That one shop changed the entire food retail culture and others had to follow. The Christian book trade was like a string of independent co-ops wedded to a specific and, unfortunately, no longer viable ethos.

"Something else I soon identified as needing to be changed was the way the two sides of the organisation operated. I would have liked to see the business side completely separate from the committee structure of the parent organisation, while, of course, covenanting it a proportion of the profits. The problem with mixing them was that business decisions were hampered by and taken in accordance with the committee ethos of the mission side. Similarly, the mission side would face problems because the publishing programme would have dominated it. If the commercial side (where my work lay) could not be allowed to reinvest our profits, we could never become the mainstream publisher SU wanted us to be. Unless there was a dramatic change in the structure of the organisation, both sides would lose out. The business would be less effective and the mission less credible.

"I fought my case but it was a battle I did not win. Sadly,

subsequent events suggest that, had the changes been made, the publishing arm of SU would have gone from strength to strength and would be a stronger force today. It would have specialised in Bible teaching, hymn books, children's literature and books for those inquiring about Christianity."

Robert is careful not to paint too gloomy a picture of his five years with SU. There were numerous successes. It's worth remembering he had only been hired on a six-month temporary contact. He shared the vision of the dedicated staff who longed, like him, to see Christ made known. He recognised the high regard in which the SU was held as an authority on Scripture. People trusted SU and that trust bred customer loyalty. He informed the trustees that if they did not change, SU would end up having to leave London, lose its shops and publicity would revert to being a problem, rather than a solution or contribution, to their mission work. "All three prophecies came true," he adds.

First, he had to improve what he saw as a major weakness, the marketing of SU material. Just as he had once advised the Co-Op to change its food labels in order to make its tins and bottles more attractive and easier to identify, so he persuaded his new bosses to adopt a similar approach for their books. For example, he felt the typeface used in the Scripture notes was too small and the notes themselves crammed full of print. There was no "air" on the page— which may not have been an issue for biblical scholars—but Robert wanted to attract ordinary Christians as well as non-Christians to Bible study. He also felt SU published too many books it could not sell. Again, a main problem was a lack of colour and attractive cover design, especially those intended for children and younger readers.

"I sent books back to the printers, demanding new covers were put on, and I then raised the price by a third. Our warehouse in Bristol was crammed with unsold stock, many marked at the same price for ten years or more. I also introduced the slip case and presentation case, another sales technique common today with major publishers, but relatively unheard of in the publishing industry at the time, certainly in the Christian media.

"One mistake that occurred before my time was probably one of the worst any company could make—opening up its business to its competitors. SU had a network of voluntary secretaries across the country who acted as agents for SU notes which were sent to them. In one act, this arrangement was ended, which meant the secretaries had to go to the bookshops for the notes and there they saw rival notes. Now they could pick and choose. From a commercial marketing point of view, SU really shot itself in the foot."

The Ladybird Bible is remembered as an unprecedented success, not only in financial terms, but also as a tool to instil a love of Scripture in young children. Parents loved reading this version to their children who also needed little encouragement to pick it up themselves. The Ladybird Bible was popular in primary schools and Sunday schools alike—and its roots lay in Robert's gift of marketing.

He persuaded Ladybird, which published a large number of best-selling children's books, to publish a Bible version. As an added incentive, he tied the book in with a TV deal to gain maximum publicity. Robert handled the sales and management; James Jones (later Bishop of Liverpool) coordinated the visuals and was an immense help to Robert in every aspect of the Ladybird Bible; and John Hunt (who went on to run his own children's publishing company) was editorial director while Jenny Robertson wrote the text and Alan Parry produced the illustrations.

The Ladybird Bible was published in twenty-four short volumes, dividing the Bible into bite-sized chunks. Yorkshire TV called the parallel series "God's Story" and ran it at various times throughout the year. More children watched the TV production "God's Story" on television than went to Sunday School.

"My lifelong aim of making the Bible's story accessible to all was being fulfilled in a fresh way," says Robert. "Unfortunately, as soon as we started work, the politics began. SU wanted editorial control as did Ladybird. I put my diplomatic hat on, telling Ladybird that if they phrased anything wrongly they would alienate potential Christian buyers and endanger any future religious titles. The SU logo on an item gave it a mark of excellence and confidence.

"As for the SU, I hoped it would promote the Ladybird Bible through Sunday schools where many of its staff worked as volunteers. My idea was for a free copy of the first volume to be given to every Sunday school in the country. Sadly, the SU attitude was that missionaries do not promote products. I could see where they were coming from, but I didn't agree. The Ladybird Bible was a major success, remaining a best-seller in W.H. Smith's children's section for ten years. It could have been a frontrunner instead of a forerunner overtaken by many excellent children's Bibles. I saw enormous potential in SU but, as time went on, many in the company just saw me as a cuckoo in the nest. They did not approve of the commercial ethos I tried to introduce.

"They were good people. I've never met anyone I've liked more who made it obvious—in the nicest possible way—that they wanted me out. I left Scripture Union with great sadness."

Paul Marsh, Publishing Director of Scripture Union, values the thirty-year friendship he has enjoyed with Robert. He describes him as an easy man to love but a difficult man to keep up with. "When we first interviewed him at Scripture Union for the position of Marketing Director, I was struck with the multiple successes he had already achieved in retailing, and the incredible enthusiasm and energy he was bringing to Scripture Union.

"My only fear was whether that enthusiasm could be channelled through such a traditional institution as Scripture Union then was. It was something of a bumpy ride, as Robert clearly set out he had little time for the committee structure involving meetings and a long haul to reach any decision, which was the way movements like Scripture Union had been traditionally run. I know Robert is the first to acknowledge his huge debt to Scripture Union and he continues to speak fondly of them and is always encouraged every time he hears of their success and progress."

Robert and Scripture Union parted company. It was indeed a sad day; but another sadness was waiting to engulf him in a way he could not have imagined.

Joyce had cancer.

Robert, Annabelle and Emily-Rose

THANK YOU, KING JAMES

Three women

It was the sort of freezing, drizzling January morning that made memories of their daughter Julia's wedding, just four months earlier, all the warmer. Robert was with Joyce at the hospital, where they were waiting for a specialist to bring the results of a series of tests. Joyce had found a lump on her leg. She had had them before and went for an annual check-up, so she was not overly concerned.

As they sat in the doctor's office, Robert thought of that glorious September day when their daughter Julia was married. Over one hundred young friends travelled up from London to their home in Bath for the wedding. They were supposed to return on the last train, but everyone was having too much fun, so they camped in the garden, or in any room there was space. Grandma was shocked to find someone sleeping in the bath when she went upstairs. In the morning, hardly a piece of carpet was visible below the stacks of cups, cake and paper hats. Joyce waltzed round the house filming the happy scene on a video camera before standing in front of the lens: "What fun! We'd do it all again," she sighed.

It was a time for celebrations. In a few months, Robert and Joyce would be marking twenty-five years of married life and Julia's new in-laws would be marking their thirtieth wedding anniversary. Sitting in the cold clean clinic, it was difficult to stay focussed on such joyful events. The surgeon, a semi-retired man, marched in briskly. He placed a file on the desk and spoke kindly and directly.

"You have a melanoma. I'm sorry to tell you it's malignant and lethal."

In the assault caused by those two short sentences, one word stuck in Robert's brain: "lethal". Joyce sat motionless. When faced with a crisis in his business life, Robert's first response was to stay calm, examine the facts and assess the situation.

"Is it curable?" he asked.

"No, I'm sorry. It has spread to the lymph system. There's very little we can do."

"Is it terminal?"

"Not yet. But it is unpredictable. It's a fast-spreading cancer."

"Is it controllable?"

"We can try. We'll do all we can."

At best, the surgeon predicted Joyce would live for six months. In fact, she survived two-and-a-half years. It was puzzling why Joyce hadn't noticed the cancer spreading, but when her medical records were checked it was discovered she had had a malignant mole removed eighteen years earlier. However, she had never been told it was malignant and was therefore unaware she should be vigilant against the cancer returning.

A few days later, a grieving father broke the news to his crying children in the room which, just a few months earlier, had been the scene of such joyful celebrations. As a child, the source of Robert's crying was hunger, fear or pain; now it was love—love for a wife and mother who had been given such devastating news. Over the next few weeks, simple everyday routines such as shopping became difficult, especially for a strong-willed woman like Joyce Hicks.

Robert said that right from the moment they heard the diagnosis, neither Joyce nor he asked the question many people ask regarding suffering: "Why me?" Their faith remained unaffected by the diagnosis or as Joyce's condition worsened. She was confident God's grace was always with her.

Robert adds: "We knew the difference between saying, 'Your will be done', and stating, 'This is your will.' Not once did Joyce place any blame at heaven's door. Joyce would quote Scripture where God explained the rain fell on both the good and the bad. Faced with illness or other misfortunes, some people blame God and grow bitter while others blame Satan and raise false expectations. Joyce did not adopt either approach but simply placed herself in God's care. She did not hide from the reality but she did make time, and time was important to her; time to be alone with herself so she could receive God's love and truth."

A few weeks later, Joyce collapsed and the family thought this was the end, but she recovered and appeared to be getting stronger. She had hepatitis which actually attacked the cancer. The doctor said it was a "normal reaction". Over the period of a few months, she had forty tumours removed, including a large one on the side of her face. Robert described it as his "favourite pecking place" but, despite the threat of disfigurement from new tumours, and even talk of plastic surgery, Joyce's faith remained strong. She was resolute in fighting cancer, but was never angry against God.

"Early on in the cancer, a Christian friend involved in a healing ministry came to pray for Joyce. She felt a heat pass through her body, but she told me she felt healed in her spirit, not her body. From that moment, all Joyce's fears for the future were removed. She knew she was in hands stronger than her own. This did not mean she simply lay down and let the cancer rule. It was a lovely paradox that Joyce was not afraid of dying, yet she fought to stay alive.

"Joyce described death as going to sleep on a cold October day and waking up in the warmth and vitality of a clear spring morning. We prayed and read the Bible together and she particularly loved and received comfort from the Psalms. She would speak beautifully about the Lord as her Shepherd. She saw herself walking with him in green pastures, smiling and full of joy. We were strengthened by good Christian friends, especially some from the Bible Society. There were cards and flowers and people dropping by for coffee. A few Christian friends kept their distance because they could not face the thought of death, but even then Joyce was patient and understanding with them and their insensitivity. We knew many, many people were praying for us, so we felt like the Apostle Paul when he was in prison and told his friends their prayers had made the difference."

Joyce was keen to try different therapies including a special fruit juice diet which Robert found difficult but he still supported his wife. The type of cancer she had meant she was in a lot of pain most days. This did not prevent her from organising weekends and seminars for cancer sufferers. On one occasion, more than fifty people, some sufferers like she was, and others who were relatives of people with cancer, packed the house. Joyce and Robert took up dry-flower arranging to raise money for other cancer friends.

Living bravely with cancer

The months flowed by and Joyce's dependable and practical manner was as strong as ever, even when she had to spend a few days in hospital having tumours removed or receiving some kind of treatment. Her great joy was witnessing the birth of two grandchildren: a daughter, Amy, to Julia and a son, Sam, to Joanna. Joyce had embraced the Psalm that God would let her see her children's children and she did.

There were days when Joyce was too ill to move from her bed. Robert would lie beside her and they cuddled each other under a blanket. Laughter and smiles were never far away, but neither were the tears for a parting that they knew would come soon. Emotional peace and a spiritual awareness found a home under an old blanket while love grew and grew.

"I realised I was falling in love with that sweet eighteen-year-old girl in that yellow dress all over again," remarks Robert. "To fall in love this way once is indeed a blessing from God. To know that love twice is a miracle. I cannot describe that feeling in words. From the beginning to the end, and everything in between, all that I received from Joyce made me realise that I was a privileged person. Joyce was always a spiritual person, with part of her spirit wanting eagles' wings to fly away. But her unassuming, practical, no-nonsense personality was what we as a family had witnessed over the years. In her last weeks, I saw the caterpillar had become a butterfly; she was undergoing a transformation before our eyes. This potential was always there, her faith, her acceptance of Jesus. However, this was something else.

"All her life, Joyce had given of herself to others. Now she was discovering herself in a way she had not before. She loved and appreciated who she was in Christ Jesus and what God's love had given her in life. It was a love she did not just believe, but experienced."

Robert and Joyce produced a series of small booklets with titles such as "Why Fear?", "Why Cry?", "Why Give Up?" and "Why Worry?" Other booklets on heaven and the meaning of love were also published. After her death, Robert sent 25,000 booklets entitled "Joyce—An Appreciation" around hospices and churches. He was inspired by the way, in those last days, Joyce rose to heights and experiences of God's love and peace that, he admits, he is still a stranger to.

Joyce battled bravely for over two-and-a-half years. In the last few weeks, her body was covered with so many tumours it was too painful to be held or cuddled; she and Robert could only hold hands. She told him if she had died after being rushed to hospital on the day when she had her first collapse, she would have been prepared to meet God then. She felt no different two-and-a-half years later.

Their last conversation in the early hours of a warm June morning was a wonderful rambling affair. They renewed their love for the thousandth time; Joyce encouraged Robert to remarry; she entrusted her parents and their children and their children's children to him. All her children were gathered round the bed. Robert held his wife's hand. Only the whirring of a fan broke the silence. There was no more need for talk. Their love surpassed words. Joyce closed her eyes and died.

At that moment, Robert knew Joyce was with the Lord. "I remembered the painting of the kind man I had seen as a child in that old church and asking the vicar in my clumsy tongue-tied way, 'Who is dis Jesus?'" The vicar explained Jesus was the man 'who loved everyone'. As I sat by her bed, I was sure Joyce was now being embraced in that love, cuddled in that love and been taken to live eternally in that love in what Christians call heaven."

Life after Joyce

After Joyce died, Robert was ready a year later to get married again. He knows that statement will shock and surprise many people. He is emphatic this desire was not based on sexual reasons; he felt his marriage had not been completed.

"Everything Joyce and I had signed up to when we made our wedding vows had not been completed," he explains. "There was still unfinished business. I was ready to prove that the relationship I should have been having with Joyce in terms of appreciation could continue even though it was with another person. I understand many people may find this a strange thing to say, but I know spouses who have suffered bereavement like I have and they felt the same as I did. It is like parents who lose a child. They feel that the bringing up of their children has not been completed. Something has interrupted the job they were given to do. They are confused because something has gone wrong. I experienced the same emotion with marriage."

A few months after Joyce's diagnosis, Robert had taken his wife on a holiday to Tenerife. Their apartment was secluded so they could spend all their time together praying, reading Scripture, talking, laughing, going on picnics on the beach—simply being a couple. It was like falling in love all over again. But Robert recognised something had changed.

"Our time in Tenerife was a beautiful time for both of us. I gave myself to Joyce in a way I don't believe I have ever given myself to another human being before. Mentally, emotionally, physically— everything was for Joyce. But I knew something else had happened. The moment Joyce got cancer and I knew she was going to die, I no longer felt married to her. I still loved her; but marriage is about life, new life and the future. Marriage is not about death.

"Why does a person feel unmarried when you've been married to your spouse for nearly thirty years? How is it that you feel something has broken, that the covenant that has been made has gone because the covenant that has been made does not go until death?"

This phenomenon was something he explored more deeply and was encouraged by the experiences of other spouses. He identified four elements to marriage: romance; responsibility; revaluation and, finally, appreciation.

Romance is that first thrill of love; in Robert's case, the beautiful girl in a yellow dress he met in Scotland. It was that time which was theirs, exclusively; a cycle ride around the Isle of Cumbrae or a late-night dinner; a period to enjoy each other's company, each other's presence without any hindrances. Romance blends into responsibility; a time to marry, blessed with children and paying a mortgage. This is a time to grow, meet challenges at home and at work. The next element is revaluation which may many couples find the most difficult to adapt to. Children become independent and leave home; work can fulfil or disappoint; in some cases, an affair happens. Or one partner may be moving in a different direction or faster in the same direction and the result is hurt, misunderstanding, neglect or sorrow. From revaluation sprouts appreciation which, in many ways, mirrors that first romance, only it is better, richer and more rewarding because its core is something deeper, not just the idealisation of that first gaze.

"I realise these are somewhat grand generalisations of marriage but this was the case for me," says Robert. "In my experience I knew I was going through a period of revaluation for many reasons. I knew that by working at this process of revaluation, trying to reduce to the minimum the negative, selfish emotions one was going through, that eventually I would enter into a relationship with Joyce that would be very sweet and very special.

"Revaluation is not saying you are falling out of love with a person, although you might actually use those words. It is saying, 'I can still do more with my life and maybe my circumstances are holding me back from doing so.' Now, the more we understand this, the more we can help each other." The negative aspect of revaluation is one can become selfish, a tension which Robert experienced.

"As Joyce and I were preparing for Julia's wedding, we described our relationship as one moving from romance to appreciation. We relished the prospect of both of us moving forward to this important stage of our marriage. As mentioned, on Julia's wedding video, my dear wife's final words were: 'What fun! We'd do it all again.' And we would have. But life does not go backwards, only forwards."

Annabelle

If Robert was ready to remarry, the big question was where should he start? A recently bereaved person is often vulnerable in different ways. A few women made it clear to Robert they were available. Some hinted at marriage, others just wanted friendship.

Robert ran from anyone who became too dominant.

Throughout his life, Robert had seen the hand of God in many of the big moments—and many of the small ones, too. He thought of the numerous times he had seen God remarkably at work: the paper and ink he needed to copy out his first Bible; the invitation by the Ainsleys to go to Scotland where he met Joyce. These and many more were times when he placed himself in God's care rather than try to pursue his own agenda. Little did Robert realise that an event was slowly being formed that would fill the hole he felt in his heart left by Joyce's death and that Mrs Ainsley would be central to its fruition.

A few months after Joyce's funeral, Robert was visiting Mrs Ainsley and talking of his future. Mrs Ainsley smiled and said she knew of a Christian woman, Annabelle, whom she thought Robert should meet.

Robert was intrigued. When he first met Annabelle he was attracted to her. His first attempts to pursue her failed, but after some months, Robert invited Annabelle to meet him at the church where he had been baptised, when he was preaching there. That evening was the start of their relationship; they were married four months later.

In Annabelle, Robert found a woman he loved and admired. She constantly surprised and delighted him. She chose a modest wedding, with some friends decorating the church, baking and decorating the wedding cake herself and making her own dress. The couple could not have been happier.

However, God had one more surprise in store for him—a major one. Three years after they married, Annabelle became pregnant, with a daughter, Emily-Rose.

Smiled Robert: "I now have a daughter younger than my grandchildren! Emily-Rose plays a major role in my life; she has brought a playfulness and innocence back to my life. I am eternally grateful to God."

Robert with images of the Millenium Gospels.

The Word around the world

In the darkness of an old kitchen cupboard, fifteen-year-old Robert Hicks desperately groped around for a book he could one day read. The Bible he found was an unknown book to him; yet within a short time, it changed his life. It would also lead to another important discovery—Church. After his outstanding success in the secular business world, Robert committed himself to making these two central pillars—the Bible and Church—better known to hundreds of millions of people still groping in the darkness for the true Light of the World.

What he has actually achieved (and more projects are still in the pipeline) has been astounding, a sure sign that God had to be involved or the whole project would never have got off the ground. Robert is the man who founded the largest single local-church invitational initiative in the world—Back to Church Sunday. In addition, he has printed and distributed across the globe over 100 million Bibles, New Testaments and Bible Selections, all beautifully printed in full colour.

Before he embarked upon these initiatives, he would use his unrivalled business experience to promote Christian media through a new company called Creative Publishing. He had left Scripture Union on good terms, but disappointed they had not acted on many of his ideas. He recognised that a large section of the Christian publishing industry lacked his vision. Now he was out on his own again, it was time to put up or shut up and, as a born entrepreneur and encourager, Robert Hicks was not someone who would ever go quietly.

"My basic desire was to encourage ordinary people to study the

Bible, its teaching and application in simple yet attractive ways. What Christians produced had to look as good and be as professional as what the secular market produced. The message of Jesus is too life-changing to be mediocre. I demanded excellence. I started hawking ideas around, offering to help package them. I attempted to get Christian publishers and ministries to produce colour editions of the Gospels or Bible, but they didn't want to know. When I suggested colour reading notes, executives looked at me as if I was mad. In the end, I felt God telling me I would have to do it myself, so I started Creative Publishing."

One idea was a personalised Gospel with a specially printed cover which could be given away at a local event. Rather than selling through the traditional book trade, Robert believed direct selling would achieve greater penetration of the market. Another innovation was the co-edition which allowed overseas publishers to insert their black and white texts into pre-colour picture Bibles. This made print-runs longer while reducing the costs per unit. Creative Publishing teamed up with the Billy Graham Evangelical Association during its 1984 and 1985 mission to England, offering the Association 100,000 copies of the Gospel of Luke for free; they ordered a further 250,000 and paid cost price. Robert was also responsible for producing a beautiful full-colour magazine for the Billy Graham Association. An initial collaboration with the leading German publishers, Brockhouse and Brunen, led to Creative accounting for fifteen per cent of their total business.

From the start, Robert wanted to work with other Christian publishers and ministries, rather than set up in competition. He regarded Creative as a hub, not a competitive marketplace, where ideas could be swapped and synergy rewarded. When some Christian companies essentially stole his ideas, he was disappointed and sad they preferred commercialisation over collaboration. But he never took action or even grumbled; in fact, he regarded it as something of a compliment and, as long as it meant more Gospels and Bibles were reaching more people, he was content to turn the other cheek and just praise God. A highly popular initiative Robert launched was a Gospel for students to be distributed by the Christian students in colleges and universities across the UK.

This project was taken up by the Universities and Colleges Christian Fellowship (UCCF). One of that group's best-known evangelists was Nigel Lee who was the man behind the Big Idea which provided quality Gospels designed for students. This scheme is now spread across one hundred countries.

Alongside, but completely separate from Creative Publishing, was Robert Frederick Publishing. Today, his two sons are in charge although they don't mind their dad dropping in with the odd idea or two. Robert Frederick is a secular commercial enterprise—and a highly successful one at that. The first year saw a small loss posted but, since then, the business has gone from strength to strength. It capitalised on quirky yet informative products such as "The Really Useful Home Book" featuring recipes and household tips. More than half a million copies were sold within three years. The profit margin was extremely high because Robert discovered the law defined stationery as having 25% of the available space for the purchaser to use. This little known fact meant other items like birthday books or address books could be published without attracting VAT.

"Robert Frederick Limited went from a standing start to becoming a dominant player in its market within five years. That was an amazing story of success. The challenge is to grow through acquisition of different types of product or by diversifying its own creative energy into other markets or other products. In the creative field, if you are successful, you will soon have imitators."

The power of the Word of God

From the first moment he read the first line of Genesis and copied it out on an old piece of spreadsheet paper, Robert recognised the power of the Bible. He read the King James Version but, over the years, he has used around twenty different translations for his own study. He says: "Reading Scripture alone, preaching on its content or studying with others, I knew that the Bible is alive; it is the living Word that spoke the universe into existence and it has a word for every situation in anyone's life. When Jesus was tempted by the devil during his forty days in the desert, the Messiah, God made man, quoted Scripture, telling the devil, 'It is written…'

"It is not just another good book or moral guide. The Bible is God speaking to his created realm throughout human history. It sets people free in every way. It brought freedom to a tongue-tied, abused boy when he was written off by society. It was the Bible which energised a ragtag group of uneducated fishermen and hated tax collectors to transform their society so that people asked, 'Who are these men who are turning the world upside down?' It was for these reasons that I did not want to waste a moment getting Gospels and the Bible into the hands of as many people as possible.

"When the Berlin Wall came down, many people saw the need to get food and other forms of aid into the former East Berlin where people had suffered so much under Communism. Even the drug dealers and pornographers moved in to set up their stalls. Well, I saw the need to get the Bible in now that restrictions had been removed.

"Creative Publishing sponsored and supported the publication of one million full-colour New Testaments. People in East Germany were hungry for the Word and I wanted to feed them. As we approached the millennium, many people were worried about the supposed Y2K bug which would allegedly bring chaos to the world's computer systems. Well, I knew the world was in chaos already as long as people did not know Jesus. That is why I teamed up with Charles Moore, the then editor of the Daily Telegraph, to give away a special Millennium Gospel. The Daily Express also ran a twelve-page supplement at the millennium which the Rev. Richard Bewes from All Souls Church in London described as 'an old fashioned scoop'.

"There was a need to make the Millennium Gospel more available, so, working with 100,000 Christians through 10,000 churches, we distributed Gospels to 25% of all UK homes. It was an awesome achievement. In all, around 100 million Bibles, Gospels and Bible Selections have gone around the globe and I am aiming at one billion before I go to be with the Lord."

Other targets included colleges and universities, not just in the UK but also overseas. This venture has now grown to over a hundred countries through the work of UCCF. Yet another initiative is "A Fresh Retelling of the Bible". The first four Gospels are now available and it is hoped over the next few years the entire Bible will be completed. The Fresh Retelling series uses visual words in order to make the historical text clearer for today's readers making it a unique bridge into the Bible for those who seldom read or have not read the Bible for a long time.

To help people with a language difficulty or barrier, Robert masterminded a user-friendly English dictionary. A particular joy for Robert was a visit to Buckingham Palace, along with Annabelle and Emily-Rose, to present a Bible on the occasion of the Queen's Jubilee. The Bible was the same text that Robert had copied out by hand forty-five years earlier, but now completely redesigned.

Now that he had launched various initiatives on the Word, he planned a radical new way to get people into churches where they could be helped in their Bible reading and understanding.

"While the Millennium Gospels were an amazing success, reports filtering back indicated one area of weakness was the personal one-to-one touch. Its one thing to give someone a Gospel, and yet another to help that Word come alive to them through a strong fellowship and communal worship—what we call church.

"I knew it was important to bring people back to church who had not been for some time, as well as reaching out to those who, for whatever reason, had never been at all. The television and the press do not present a very positive image of church or believers in general. Many people have no idea what happens on a Sunday morning. I prayed long over this and the Lord made it clear to me it was time to bring people back and that led me to launch a new campaign called Back to Church Sunday.

"The idea was unique but simple. If every churchgoer asked one person in a year to come to church, the national effect would be amazing."

Robert spoke with the pastor, Rev. Alan Bain, and members of St Philip and St James church in his home town of Bath about this new initiative. They were enthusiastic, immediately recognising its potential. Bath and Worthing were the first churches to sign up to Back to Church Sunday. When the project was picked up by the Diocese of Manchester, it simply snowballed. Christians identified it as a people-friendly way to reach the mass of the population, whether in their own homes, in the workplace or over the garden fence. BTCS was neither threatening nor boring and assured everyone of a warm, friendly welcome. The project was universal but organic so individual churches could devise events suited to their own area or culture. Robert has special praise for his close friend of some thirty years, Gerald Thompson, with whom he worked closely on Back to Church resources which were created and printed in Kosovo where Gerald set up a printing business to help strengthen relations between the small Christian community and its larger

Muslim community. For the first time in that country's history, a Bible Sunday was established among the growing church.

Today BTCS it truly is a worldwide outreach, the largest of its kind, operating in regions such as America, Australia, Canada, South America, across Europe and numerous African nations. It is also extremely trans-denominational having been adopted by the Church of England, Salvation Army, Baptists, Elim, United Reformed, the Church in Wales and Churches Together in Scotland. The Church of England figures alone for 2009 show 53,000 people were welcomed back, a 71% increase on the previous year. Worldwide, an estimated one million people have gone back to church.

"With more churches and more nations taking up the plan, those figures will surely rise year on year," adds Robert. "The Lord is truly doing a mighty work."

Robert's latest project is called "Open Your Bible", a new approach which uses online resources including a website. But whatever the method, he has one aim—to make the Bible more accessible to more people every day.

*****

Robert Hicks has come full circle. Yet he continues to push forward. As he approaches his eighth decade, his determination to put the Bible into more hands and hearts is undiminished. He has the same hunger to learn, teach and share the Word that he had at fifteen when he first discovered Scripture. He has the same imagination as when he lay beside Frankley Beeches Reservoir and in his mind's eye saw the Spirit hover over the water; it is that imagination which is the source of ever new ideas to make the Bible fresh and accessible. He retains the same belief that the Bible will set people free, as it set him free from a life of poverty, abuse and isolation. He wants others to be blessed, whether in marriage, with children or in business—in fact in however God calls them to live their life. He has the same certainty that, whatever sadness and tragedy enters into one's life, God's Word brings comfort and peace, joy and solace, certainty and truth.

His mission is to take the Bible to the world so that millions more people have the opportunity one day to walk through pastures green with the very Author himself.

It is a mission he has been committed to ever since as an awkward, semi-literate teenager, he took a piece of paper, an old ink pen and opened a book called The Holy Bible.

A number of years ago, Robert received a request to lead the funeral of a man who lived at No. 335 Stonehouse Lane after the Hicks had moved out. After the service, the man's children approached him, holding something he only half remembered from a time long, long ago.

"It was a wooden box, the same wooden box which covered the gas meter which I used as a table on which to copy out the Bible," he explains. "The house was about to be renovated and workmen were tearing out the gas meters and dumping them. They knew of my story and decided to save the box and present it to me. I was overcome with emotion. I couldn't believe it. So many memories flooded back, of how I hunched over that box night after night for months, copying out and trying to speak God's Word in that cold kitchen.

"Above all, I marvelled at how God had used me, the least likely of people, to help spread his Word across the world. I have that old wooden box now in my living room. It is a constant reminder that God's grace truly is amazing.

"If God can use me, he can use anyone."

A copy of the King James Version of the Bible.

Epilogue

The man carrying the old telephone directories was quickly surrounded by a huge, expectant crowd. Even the two street evangelists joined the circle that formed round him on Birmingham's famous Bull Ring were keen to see what he would do.

This part of the Ring was popular with buskers of every type who performed to Saturday shoppers and tourists. The man was cracking jokes as he urged the crowd to make a tighter circle. His deeply-tanned, muscular arms and face were evidence he was used to performing outdoors. His manner was confident and funny. As the crowd jostled, the man made a face, pointing to his upturned hat lying on the ground, and reminded his audience to be generous. People laughed.

Placing a finger to his lips, he stared solemnly at the crowd; his face hummed with concentration. Flexing his powerful arms, the man picked up one of his telephone directories which he balanced on his knee. Slowly, he started to tear the book in two. The vast muscles in his arms bulged, his breathing grew stronger and the telephone book began to rip apart to the onlookers' astonishment. Seconds later, there was a shredding noise and then the man held the two torn pieces above his head. The crowd clapped and cheered.

Throwing the mangled pieces on the ground, the busker noticed Robert standing nearby, a large black book tucked under his arm.

"Hey, is that a Bible, son?" he asked loudly.

Everyone looked across to where Robert was standing with his friend. The pair had been out doing street evangelism that morning. The young men, who attended a local church, believed God was calling them to this public witness.

"Yes," Robert replied. "It's my Bible."

"Are you a Christian?"

"Yes, I am."

The busker put his hands on his hips, smiling broadly. He asked: "Do you believe Jesus when he said it is better to give than to receive?"

"I do. I'm delighted to see you know Jesus and the Bible."

"Would you give me your Bible, then? I don't have one."

The crowd may have thought this conversation was part of the act. They hung on every word, watching the cocky busker and the equally confident young man he had picked out from their midst.

The busker asked again: "Well? If you believe it is better to give than receive, will you give me your Bible?"

Robert's fingers wrapped round his Bible. He knew the Word of God was not just paper and ink bound in book form. The Bible was alive. But the Bible he was holding was very special to him.

He remembered the first time his fingers had felt its cool leather binding as he reached far into the recess of a living room cupboard at No. 335 Stonehouse Lane. He remembered pulling it out, brushing off a layer of dust and grime, so that its gold edges glittered in the candlelight. He remembered polishing the cover with shoe polish until it gleamed. He thought about the first time he read the opening line of Genesis and copied the words on to the blank side of used spreadsheet paper.

Over the years, Robert had marked passages and highlighted phrases. Favourite Scriptures were underlined and an assortment of bookmarks gave easy access to well-used verses. This book had helped bring Robert to the Lord and out of an abusive silence.

"Well," repeated the busker. "Will you let me have your Bible?"

"Yes. But only if you promise to read it and not tear it in half. God's Word is powerful and should be respected. It will change your life."

"I promise," replied the man.

Robert stepped forward and handed over his precious Bible. The man smiled, shook his hand then lifted his unused telephone directories off the ground. Scooping up his hat full of money, he disappeared through the crowd.

Afterword: the Hicks siblings today

Robert gives an update on his brothers and sisters, some of whom he never met.

The Twins

If my research is correct, my mother gave birth to twins while in her teens. None of my family has ever met them. My prayer is that they found security with their adoptive parents and that these parents laid a foundation of love and encouragement, so that when the time came for them to establish their own families, it would have been as normal and happy as ours should have been.

Donald

My eldest half-brother, Donald, was devastated when, after twenty-eight years, his mother returned. As a child, she promised she would never leave him, but she did and stayed out of contact for so long. There were no birthday or Christmas cards. After spending an unjustifiable time in Borstal, he joined the army where he rose to the rank of sergeant. He met and married Janice and they raised their happy family in Devizes. Janice believes the shock of his mother's return triggered the decline in Donald's heath. He developed diabetes, lost the sight in one eye and had part of his foot amputated. When he spent time in a hospital near me, we got to know each other and enjoyed each other's company. He had firm political convictions and was a proud, independent man. Donald died from a sudden heart-attack. My tears at his funeral were heartfelt even though we had only grown to know each other in his final year.

John

John, or Jack, was my asthmatic brother who cycled alongside mother's bus when she left us. He was clever, handsome and with a natural charm. Like me, Jack left school without any qualifications. He struggled with his asthma, being placed in various institutions for lengthy periods, and found it difficult to get a proper education. He also bore many scars from our home life. Donald married Pam and they raised a family together, but sadly they divorced. He later found love and happiness with a lovely lady called Margaret. I wish them many happy years together.

Jean

Her life is a story in itself. As the only girl in the family with a father who robbed her of so much, Jean faced many mountains to overcome. Jean became pregnant in her teens but the child's father abandoned her. When she was pregnant for the third time, her husband, Lloyd, tragically died. Jean later nursed a companion through illness until he also died. Except for her first child, all her children are of mixed race. Jean brought up all her children almost singlehandedly and with unbelievable dramas along the way. She has come through it all marvellously. She has proved beyond doubt that she has nothing to be ashamed of. I have said it before and I will always say it: Jean is my hero.

Bernard

In recent years, my younger brother, Bernard, has become a real friend. Like Jack, he suffered from asthma and, like Jean, a squint which was not remedied until he was twenty-one. Bernard married Sue and they had two children, but, sadly, the marriage ended in divorce. However, I have never heard Bernard speak a single word against his former wife. He has come through many crises and, for a time, shared his home with a lady whom he married in hospital a few days before she died. Sadly, Bernard died of a heart-attack. His death has left a large void in my heart.

Brian

I vividly remember the day I found Brian after he'd been beaten terribly with a fender by father. He suffered bullying at school and, even today, cannot read or write. Brian describes himself as the black sheep of the family which is not, and never has been, true. He had two children with his partner. Brian tried desperately to rekindle a relationship with mother when she returned, but it was difficult. Brian has become a loving brother and true friend.

Two half-sisters—unknown

Two half-sisters, one born 1946 and one in 1952. I never met either. I do pray for them and hope they have had a full life with good parents.

Comments from family and friends

A portrait of Bobby by Mr Henry Mee, the distinguished portrait artist of royalty, captains of industry and other celebrities, hangs at the entrance to the students' library of Birmingham University. If the thousands and thousands of students who visit the library were to discover the story of the early years of the man, I am sure they would be motivated to put to good use the privileges and gifts that have come their way and would also want to help the under-privileged who have so much less. We are all very proud of Bobby and hope his story is read and appreciated by many people.
—Bernard Hicks, younger brother

Bobby was definitely the quiet one of the family, and was always thinking. Looking back, I realise that there were leadership qualities in him. Bobby was also hard-working which is why he succeeded in business, but it was impossible for us as children, or even as adults, to realise he would be so successful in so many different ways. I am sure that people who read Bobby's story for themselves will be as surprised as we are in his own family.
—Brian Hicks, youngest brother

I well remember Bobby writing in his corner of our small living room, using the wooden cover that hid the gas meter as his desk. He started educating himself by copying out the Bible by hand. His powers of concentration were incredible and he spent hour after hour copying the text which, when he began, he could not read properly. I am so proud of how he overcame his lack of education, his speech difficulties and his dyslexia. Above all, I am so proud of who he has turned out to be.
—Jeanette Hicks, sister

One of the many memories we all have is the amount of time our dad gave to us, even though he worked long hours plus a further hour travelling to his office. He would come home from work, undoubtedly tired and exhausted, and find all four of us children

already in bed. Dad always came straight upstairs to engage us in one of his magical adventure stories which would captivate our imagination. From downstairs, we would hear mum shout: "Bob, your dinner's getting cold!" Dad would continue to thrill us with his stories. Mum would shout again: "Bob, your dinner's getting cold." We sat entranced by dad's story. Eventually, the voice downstairs would announce: "Bob, your dinner is cold."
—Joanna Hicks, daughter

During his time as a member of Bethany, Bob was an inspirational Bible teacher. His notoriety soon extended further afield and he was much sought after across Wirral and Merseyside for his ministry and teaching. He excelled in commencing Bible projects such as compact Bible Schools. Bob was a founder member of the Way for Wirral tent crusades. He also organised a period of practical experience for over one hundred students from Capernwray Hall to work alongside a dozen churches in their communities. We commend Bob for the strong biblical foundation of his faith and his highly developed and innovative skills as a Bible teacher, allied to his long experience of Christian work and service.
—The elders of Bethany Chapel, Prenton, Wirral

Being a Londoner who has viewed life at its most raw, I have become accustomed to the difficult parts of life. But I am in awe at how Robert survived his childhood with the abuse, his dyslexia and being tongue-tied. I remember when he first came into publishing, how he revolutionised a lot of thinking because of his professional marketing approach. I am constantly amazed at the whole range of enterprises he initiates, sponsors and encourages.
—Alan Bain, friend and BBC producer and presenter

I invited Bob to be the guest speaker at the celebration of the Golden Wedding for myself and my wife, Sheila. You can imagine my surprise to discover that, the following week, he would be making a presentation at Buckingham Palace for Her Majesty the Queen during the celebrations of her Golden Jubilee. He was to present a

Commemoration Jubilee Bible in the same King James text that Bob had copied out in his teens. Bob is an encourager to many, a family man and, of course, a successful man in more ways than one. I can only stand back and acknowledge that such achievements were made possible by a power outside of himself—God. I have no hesitation in commending the story of Bob Hicks to you all.

—Aubrey Marks former Midlands Manager for the UK's largest dairy company

I have known Robert for twenty-five years. He is one of the most creative, passionate and dedicated friends I have. The words, "But we've always done it that way", are not in his vocabulary. Robert is always searching for new and different ways to reach people— unchurched as well as churched—with the Word of God and encourage them to read it. He believes strongly that it is the Word that will change people's lives and the application of scriptural truths will enable the believer to rejoice at God's blessing and find help in times of hardship.

—Lawrence M Stone, Vice President and Publisher of Rutledge Hill Press, Nashville

Robert (left) with Charles Moore

Robert (right) with publishing director for Billy Graham UK crusades

Robert and Joyce on their wedding day

Robert and Joyce with grandchildren Amy and Sam

A portrait of Robert hanging in the Library of Birmingham University